JAMES
GARFIELD

PRESIDENTIAL ✦ LEADERS

JAMES GARFIELD

RUTH TENZER FELDMAN

⌐ LERNER PUBLICATIONS COMPANY / MINNEAPOLIS

To Jane

Lerner Publications Company
A division of Lerner Publishing Group
241 First Avenue North
Minneapolis, MN 55401 U.S.A.

Website address: www.lernerbooks.com

Library of Congress Cataloging-in-Publication Data

Feldman, Ruth Tenzer.
    James Garfield / by Ruth Tenzer Feldman.
       p.   cm.
    Includes bibliographical references and index.
    ISBN: 0–8225–1398–6 (lib. bdg. : alk. paper)
    1. Garfield, James A. (James Abram), 1831–1881—Juvenile literature. 2. Presidents—United States—Biography—Juvenile literature. I. Title.
    E687.F45   2005
    973.8'4'092—dc22   2004019764

Manufactured in the United States of America
1 2 3 4 5 6 – JR – 10 09 08 07 06 05

CONTENTS

———— ✧ ————

*James A. Garfield had a dramatic life working on the
Ohio and Pennsylvania Canal as a teenager.*

INTRODUCTION

I was beginning to grow reckless.
—James Garfield,
letter to his mother, November 1855

Autumn 1848. It was about midnight when the canal boat *Evening Star* edged toward a lock along the Ohio and Pennsylvania Canal. Still drowsy from sleep, sixteen-year-old James Abram Garfield stumbled onto the deck. He had recently been promoted from a job guiding the mules that pulled the canal boat through the locks to a job as a "bower." His duty was to stand at the narrow front (bow) of the boat and guide the *Evening Star* through the canal.

James, dressed in a heavy oilcloth coat and pants, slipped off the wet deck and fell into the canal. Although nearly six feet tall and very strong, he was not particularly agile. And as he later admitted, "I could not swim a particle and I knew almost nothing about the water except what I had read."

James grabbed for a rope hanging over the boat, hoping to hoist himself out of the water. Instead of holding taut, the rope began to unwind. Here's how he told the story:

I felt I was coming to drowning. At length, however, [the rope] held and I was able to draw myself up until I could get a breath of air above the stagnant, stifling water. . . . My feeble calls for help [received] no response from the sleeping people upon the boat. I at length made a great struggle and drew myself upon the boat. I was curious to know what had caused the rope to stop unwinding and carefully examining it, I found that just where it came over the edge of the boat it had been drawn into a crack and there knotted itself. I sat down in the cold of the night and in my wet clothes and [thought about] the matter. . . . I thought [God] had saved me for my mother and for something greater and better than canaling.

By the next morning, James had changed his mind. This was the fourteenth time he had fallen into the canal, and somehow he had managed to survive. Restless for adventure and eager to see the world, James wasn't ready to return to life with his mother on their small farm in Ohio. "My strong will had settled upon the life of a sailor," he wrote, "and it would be difficult to break it."

CHAPTER ONE

EARLY TIMES IN OHIO

Jas. A Garfield's daily Register.
January first 1848.
Preface.

It being New Year's day I commence a journal
of the general events of my life. The object of
this little work is to exercise the hand a little
every day in writing and also to assist in
remembering events that are of some importance.

—James Garfield,
diary entry, January 1, 1848

James Abram Garfield was born on November 19, 1831, near Lake Erie, in Orange Township (later renamed Moreland Hills), Ohio. James was named after a brother who had been born in 1827 and who died two years later. He had two sisters—Mehitabel "Hitty," born in 1821, and Mary, born in 1824—and one brother, Thomas, born in

1822. James was the last and, his mother once wrote, "the largest Babe I ever had."

LIFE IN A LOG CABIN

James Garfield was born in a log cabin that nestled between two brooks that flowed into Chagrin River. James's parents, Abram Garfield and Eliza Ballou Garfield, had a small farm. They were part of Orange Township's tight-knit community of about three hundred people, not far from Cleveland, a bustling town of nearly one thousand.

Garfield's first home was a log cabin in Orange Township, not far from Cleveland, Ohio.

Abram Garfield fought a forest fire that threatened to destroy their home when James was two years old. Abram died two days later, probably from pneumonia. James's mother, at the age of thirty-one, was left with four young children. She and Thomas, who was only ten, resolved to save the farm.

They struggled through that first winter. Then they sold fifty acres of the farm to pay debts and kept the remaining thirty. The Widow Garfield took in sewing, spinning, and washing in exchange for shoes, cotton fabric, and groceries. Thomas left school and helped with the farm. He also earned twenty to twenty-five cents a day—usually paid in fruits and vegetables—by working for other farm families.

Hitty and Mary also worked hard on the farm. James, however, was the baby of the family, seven years younger than his next oldest sibling. He spent much of his early years playing and doing easier chores, such as picking fruit. He later recalled "wearing blue cotton pants rolled above my knees and wading in to 'Big Brook'. . . . I can feel the soft mud rolling up between my toes now and the 'shiners' nibbling at my shins."

The family attended meetings at the Disciples of Christ Church a few miles from the farm. James's mother was a devout member of the church and often read the Bible to the children and sang hymns. By the time James was three, he had started to read from her Bible on his own. While Thomas worked to support the family, Hitty and Mary took James to school.

James's first school was about a mile and a half away from home, in a village with a blacksmith shop and a store. Eliza Garfield was determined to have her children closer to her, so that they could work on the farm and go to school. She gave a small piece of her land to the township and had a schoolhouse built there. The schoolhouse was open to all the neighboring children. The township paid a schoolmaster to teach there for as many months a year as farmwork allowed the children to attend.

According to one Garfield family story, James just would not sit still when he first went to his new school. He squirmed and fidgeted and made a general nuisance of himself. Once he was told to go home and he did, racing back again within a few minutes because the farmhouse was so close. The schoolmaster met with James's mother and announced that he could do nothing with the boy. That night she sat James down and explained that if he wanted to go to school he had to behave himself. He agreed and with great effort managed to keep his restlessness in check. James amazed the schoolmaster with his reading ability, and at the end of the term, he received a copy of the New Testament as a prize for being the best reader in school. By the time he was eight, James had learned Webster's spelling book almost by heart.

In 1837 Hitty, aged sixteen, married Stephen Trowbridge. The couple moved to the nearby town of Solon. Thomas was often away earning money, leaving James at home with his mother and Mary. In later letters, Garfield describes this period in his life as chaotic, a time when he often ran wild. He grew strong and fearless, eager for fun, clumsy with an axe (causing many a wound), and ready to fight even someone larger than himself.

When James was ten in 1841, he offered to leave school to go to work, the way Thomas had. Thomas insisted that

A construction job on the family farm got young James (left) interested in a career as a carpenter.

James stay home with the women on the farm and continue his education.

TEENAGE DREAMS

In the fall of 1843, Thomas returned from a job in Michigan with enough money to build a new house on the farm. James helped with construction and found out he enjoyed working with the tools and timber. Then and there, he decided to become a carpenter. In 1844 his sister Mary married Marenus Larabee and joined Hitty in Solon. Thomas was often away from home, leaving James and his mother in their new house.

As a teenager, James was eager to leave the farm and find work elsewhere. He read and reread whatever he could get his hands on, including one of his favorite books, Daniel Defoe's 1719 adventure story, *Robinson Crusoe.* Another favorite was William Grimshaw's 1830 book, *The Life of Napoleon.*

Current news from across the nation started reaching Ohio as well. In 1844 Samuel Morse invented the telegraph. This invention allowed newspapers to receive up-to-date

✧ ————————

The novel Robinson Crusoe *fired James's imagination. This illustration is from a late 1700s edition of the novel.*

reports from all parts of the country. Soon newspapers started wire services to collect and print the latest telegraphed news. One of these newspapers was likely the *Cleveland Plain Dealer,* founded about then.

The big national news in 1846 was the declaration of war against Mexico in a dispute over Texas, a former province of Mexico that had just become part of the United States. James wanted to be a soldier, but he stayed near home to help his mother with the farm.

In 1847 James earned money by building an addition to the home of a blacksalter—someone who made potash, a chemical compound used mainly in fertil-izer. The saltery produced potash

Samuel Morse

by filtering water through wood ashes. Against his mother's wishes, James decided to live with the man and work in his saltery for nine dollars a month plus board. The job didn't last long. One day someone referred to James as a servant. He quit and returned to the farm.

On January 1, 1848, James started a journal. He noted his thoughts in small, neat handwriting on plain blank paper ruled for business accounts. He was a restless and active young man, eager to leave rural Ohio and see the world. His mother said James was a son who "never was still a minute at a time in his whole life." James continued to take odd jobs. In his journal, he noted that he chopped wood for a month at fifty cents a day, he washed sheep, and he cut grass for fifty cents an acre. But soon he resolved to be a sailor.

A SAILOR'S LIFE

As he recalled later: "Nautical novels did it. I had read a large number of them, all I could get in the neighborhood. My mother tried to turn my attention in other directions, but the books were considered bad and from that very fact were fascinating."

James devoured Charles Ellms's *The Pirate's Own Book or Authentic Narratives of the Lives and Executions of the Most Celebrated Sea Robbers*. The book "became a sort of bible or general authority with me."

In the spring of 1848, James chopped one hundred cords of wood on a farm within sight of Lake Erie and "the passage of a ship made me almost insane with delight." That summer he gathered up a few belongings and left for Cleveland "with the firm intention of beginning at the bottom of the business of sailing and carefully mastering it."

By this time, Cleveland had grown to a thriving port of nearly seventeen thousand people. But when James arrived there, none of the sailing vessels were at the docks, except one owned by a drunken captain, who cursed at James for bothering him. So James found a job with his cousin, Amos Lechter, whose boat, the *Evening Star,* traveled the waterways of the Ohio and Pennsylvania Canal.

James started so far down in the sailing business that most of the time he wasn't even on his cousin's canal boat. Instead, he guided the horses or mules that pulled the *Evening Star* through the waterways to Beaver, Pennsylvania, where a steamboat towed the canal boat into Pittsburgh. The *Evening Star* brought iron, copper ore, wood, and salt into that great industrial hub and returned with coal from Pennsylvania mines.

James loved life on the canal, even though he often fell in and couldn't swim. As he put it, he was "ripe for ruin" and ready to "drink in every species of vice." James was set on having a sailor's life.

After about two months on the canal, however, James became ill with a high fever and what was called ague—malaria—and could no longer work on the canal boat. One of his cousins brought him home to a grateful mother.

————————————— ✧ —————————————

From the shore of the Ohio and Pennsylvania Canal,
James urges horses to tow his cousin's canal boat.

The doctors treated him with what he described as "terrible doses of calomel," a compound of mercury and chlorine that cause severe bowel movements. "Only my powerful constitution could have saved me," he later wrote. It took four months for James to regain his health.

While recovering, James met Samuel Bates, who taught at the schoolhouse on their farm during the winter of 1848–1849. Samuel had attended Geauga Academy, a small school in Chester, and he taught in Orange Township to earn money for his tuition and expenses at the academy. He invited James, who had done well in his studies at the schoolhouse, to join him at Geauga when he returned there in the spring.

Eliza Garfield wanted her younger son to have an education, but James was still stuck on sailing. Finally, he agreed to go to school in the spring term and return to Cleveland's docks in the summer.

Geauga seemed like a good opportunity, but James was unsure of his health and abilities. He traveled to the nearby town of Bedford to see J. P. Robinson, a well-respected doctor. James asked Dr. Robinson to give him a physical examination and test his mental capabilities. The doctor did so and pronounced James capable of attending the academy.

That settled it. In March 1849, James set out for the academy with his friend Orrin Judd, his cousin William Boynton, and teacher Samuel Bates. James wore homespun clothes and took seventeen dollars, all the money that his mother and older brother Thomas could scrape together.

James Abram Garfield was once again off to seek his fortune. This was worth a journal entry. It was an event "of some importance."

CHAPTER TWO

FROM PUPIL TO POLITICIAN

I feel the necessity of breaking the shell of local notions and getting mentally free.
—James Garfield,
letter to future wife, Lucretia Rudolph, July 30, 1854

According to historians, about ninety thousand people rushed to California's newly discovered goldfields in 1849 hoping to strike it rich. But for all his wanderlust, James A. Garfield left home for an education rather than gold.

Geauga Academy was a small school, with about eight teachers and 252 students. James used his seventeen dollars to rent a room he shared with two other students, buy a woodstove, and hire a woman to prepare meals. He paid tuition and bought books at the academy. By the end of the month, there was only $1.48 left.

"I lament sorely that I was born to poverty," Garfield later wrote. "Let us never praise poverty, for a child at least."

GETTING BY AT GEAUGA

James earned his way at the academy by cutting wood for the faculty, teaching courses to other students as soon as he mastered a subject, and doing farm chores. He was sometimes embarrassed by his homespun clothes and felt snubbed by students richer than he.

But he loved school. During the first term, he took algebra, philosophy, grammar, and singing. He joined the literary society to practice his writing and public speaking. He spent hours researching topics in the academy's 150-book library. James worked at home during part of the summer and returned to school in early August to tackle his studies. His main interest during the second term was debating, and his first formal debate was in August 1849. The topic was "Are the causes that tend to strengthen greater than those which tend to dissolve the American Union?"

This question was not just an academic exercise. The United States had acquired California and other territories in the West as a result of its war with Mexico, which had ended in the spring of 1848. The question of whether slavery would be permitted in the former Mexican territories drew heated arguments on both sides.

Debates over slavery were so fierce that people had formed the abolitionist (antislavery) Free Soil Party because they were dissatisfied with the other presidential candidates in the 1848 election. By August 1849, fifteen states allowed slavery and fifteen didn't. California's political leaders wanted to gain statehood as quickly as possible and enter the Union as a free state—one prohibiting slavery. This would upset the delicate balance between free states and slave states in Congress and bring conflict over slavery to the boiling point.

The Free Soil candidate for U.S. president in 1848 was Martin Van Buren (left). Charles F. Adams ran for vice president (right). Their motto was "Free Soil, Free Labor, Free Speech."

─────────── ✧

When he returned to Geauga Academy that August, James had six cents. He wrote: "This I threw into the church contribution box on Sunday for luck and started in." James got a job putting siding on a house. He earned seventy-five cents for every one hundred feet of siding. He also taught in the local schools for a few months at a time. On November 19, 1849, he noted in his journal: "This morning I am 18 years old. Rather young to have the care of a school consisting of a company of youth, several of whom are older than myself." James, however, earned the grudging respect of his students by beating up an older boy who had driven off the previous schoolmaster.

Schoolmaster Garfield

When James Garfield taught school in the 1840s and 1850s, children went to school only a few months a year, if at all. Farm chores came first, and there was little time for school during planting and harvesting seasons. Students went to school when they could, generally in the summer and the winter. They often crammed into a single room, sometimes with girls on one side and boys on the other. These schoolhouses often had a stove, a water bucket, and not much furniture. Reading, grammar, spelling, arithmetic, and penmanship were the most common subjects. Students also memorized essays or poems and had spelling contests.

Public elementary schools had been formally established in Ohio in 1825. No public high schools existed in the state until passage of the Ohio School Law of 1849. Before then students had to pay tuition at private academies. Most students in Ohio, as elsewhere, didn't receive more than an eighth-grade education, and many received less than that.

Garfield's experience with beating up an older student was not unusual, especially in rural schools. Older boys often challenged the schoolmaster and sometimes barred the door of a schoolhouse before he came. If the schoolmaster was able to get into the school, classes would start. If he wasn't, school would be canceled for the day.

THE ECLECTIC LIFE

In March 1850, James left his teaching position. That same month, he officially joined the Disciples of Christ Church, the same denomination he attended with his mother. The Disciples had founded a school of their own—Western Reserve Eclectic Institute (later called Hiram College)—in Hiram, Ohio. James decided to continue his education there. He attacked his studies wholeheartedly, determined to be the best in all his classes, including Greek and Latin.

Public speaking and debate became his passion. James developed an elegant style of speaking, which he used both in the lecture hall and at church. One classmate who

The Western Reserve Eclectic Institute was a new college when James began to attend classes there. It was founded in 1850.

THE WESTERN RESERVE

When the first English settlers came to the New World, they had no idea how big North America really was. The British king's charter (grant) of land to the colony of Connecticut described a parcel of land that stretched from the Atlantic coast across "all the breadth . . . throughout all the main lands there, from the western ocean to the South Seas." Pennsylvania and other colonies had similar charters that only vaguely described a western boundary.

By the time of the American Revolution (1775–1783), Connecticut colonists had settled in western territory also claimed by Pennsylvania. In 1778, during the American Revolution, British troops and their Native American allies attacked one community of these colonists and brutally massacred hundreds of them. Connecticut later established its present western border. It gave up claims to the remaining land to the U.S. Congress, except for a 120-mile strip of fertile farmland along the southern shore of Lake Erie. Connecticut claimed that these lands were compensation for the survivors of the British raid. The territory was called the Western Reserve of Connecticut in Ohio. The Western Reserve later became a county in Ohio, which became a state in 1803.

admired his preaching was Lucretia Rudolph, the petite, shy daughter of one of the founders of the institute. A year younger than James, she was attracted to this tall, muscular young man with curly brown hair and piercing blue eyes.

To pay for his education, James worked as the janitor at Eclectic, cleaning the rooms, building fires to heat them, and ringing the school bell. He taught in local schools again and seemed to enjoy the experience as little as he had during his first teaching jobs. In one three-month assignment, he found himself in Blue Rock, Ohio, "in a miserable old log schoolhouse . . . as smutty as a blacksmith's shop."

James worked when he had to, returned to his mother on the farm from time to time, and stayed on at Eclectic for three years. He continued to preach, write in his journal, and refine his view and opinions of his expanding world.

Some of his opinions, such as those about the value of an education, he held for the rest of his life. Others proved to be temporary. During the presidential campaign of 1852, James wrote in his journal: "I am exceedingly disgusted with the wire-pulling of politicians and the total disregard of truth in all their operations." He was glad that he was not quite old enough to vote on November 2, 1852. He was seventeen days shy of twenty-one. Politics, he decided, was not for him.

Preaching seemed like a possible career, though. "After I get to speaking," he wrote, "I feel very calm and collected. I know not why." The Disciples Church did not have ordained ministers. Anyone with the proper learning and the inclination to serve could lead a congregation. The members of the church seemed to like James's sermons.

After about two years, James had taken almost all the courses Eclectic had to offer. He started a class of his own in penmanship, charging each pupil about a dollar to attend. He became interested in a young woman at the institute but broke off the relationship in the spring of 1853 when she became too serious.

By then James's brother Thomas had married and wanted to move to Michigan. In October 1853, the Garfields gathered at the old farm for the last time. James's mother moved in with her daughter Mary in Solon, Ohio, and James was on his own.

James turned toward Lucretia, the reserved young woman who had been a part of his circle of friends. He started to write letters to her, addressing her as his "much respected sister," and nicknamed her "Crete." But James was restless to leave Ohio. He wanted to continue his education in New England. The board of trustees graduated him from Hiram and gave him fifty dollars.

WILLIAMS AND A WIDER WORLD

In the summer of 1854, James Garfield said good-bye to Lucretia and his family. He left Ohio on a Lake Erie steamer bound for Buffalo, New York, then made his way to Williams College, in Williamstown, Massachusetts.

✧ —————————
Lucretia Rudolph

*One of Garfield's mentors at Williams College (above) was its president,
Mark Hopkins. In Hopkins's first address as president in 1836, he said, "We
are to regard the mind, not as . . . a receptacle into which knowledge may be
poured; but as a flame that is to be fed, as an active being that must be
strengthened to think and to feel—and to dare, to do, and to suffer."*

———————————— ✧ ————————————

He mistakenly arrived a month before the school term
started, but he immediately set to work improving his
knowledge of mathematics—one of his weaker subjects.

Garfield was determined to succeed. "I almost feel that
there are but two courses before me," he wrote to a friend
back home, "to stand at least among the first or die. I
believe I can do it, if granted a fair trial."

When school started, Garfield entered as a junior. With
a roommate from Hiram, he settled in at Number 16,
South College, and set to work. The instructors at Williams

College set a staid, conservative, strict tone, unlike the friendlier, supportive Disciples instructors at Eclectic. Garfield went to chapel in the morning, then recited Latin for an hour before going to breakfast. During the day, there were classes in philosophy, mechanics (physics), and Greek, then prayers again in the evening. The next term, classes included chemistry, mechanics, and German.

Garfield became a leader among those students who hadn't joined fraternities. He was elected an editor of the *Williams Quarterly*, the college's literary magazine. He engaged in political debates about whether slavery should be allowed in Kansas, the role of the Roman Catholic Church in the United States, and the dangers of immigration.

Garfield toured parts of New England while he was at Williams College. He went on fishing expeditions and visited relatives who lived nearby. During one winter break, he taught penmanship at a school in North Pownal, Vermont.

In May 1856, Garfield, who had performed well on his exams, won the honor of speaking at graduation. He invited Lucretia to his graduation and wrote to her: "I want very much to talk with you in reference to my future course of life and my duty in regard to choosing some calling."

BACK TO OHIO

Lucretia and others convinced Garfield to return to Ohio to teach at his old school. Wanting to stay in New England, Garfield reluctantly accepted a job teaching literature and ancient languages at Western Reserve Eclectic Institute for one year. He turned down an offer to become a preacher at the Disciples Church in Hiram.

It was not unusual for a professor of ancient languages to be able to write in Greek and Latin. But Garfield could write in both of these languages at the same time! Naturally left handed, he had been trained to write with his right hand as well. So while he wrote in Greek with one hand, he simultaneously wrote in Latin with the other.

In the spring of 1857, Garfield accepted the top position at Eclectic, essentially becoming its president. In addition to teaching classes, he began to preach there and to raise money for the school.

On November 11, 1858, in a small ceremony with family and a few friends, James Abram Garfield married Lucretia Rudolph. They settled into a boardinghouse in Hiram. It looked like Garfield was back in Ohio to stay.

One month later, Garfield and a philosopher, William Denton, drew a crowd of nearly one thousand people to Chagrin Falls, Ohio, for a five-day debate. Garfield gave twenty speeches, each thirty minutes long, on the role of God in the creation of life on earth. English naturalist Charles Darwin had first

——————————— ✧
The English naturalist Charles Darwin lived from 1809 to 1882. His theories of evolution remain controversial in modern times.

presented his theories of evolution to a group of scientists that year, and "Darwinism" became the hot topic of the day.

Denton argued that "[m]an, animals and vegetables came into existence by the laws of spontaneous generation and progressive development, and there is no evidence that there was ever any exertion of a direct creative power on this planet." Garfield argued against the position and decided that he had won. He later expanded his speeches into a lecture series titled "Geology and Religion."

Garfield also expressed his support for abolishing slavery. Unlike his early student days, when he didn't even want to vote, Garfield became interested in politics and in the Republican Party. He began to read law books. "I made my study of the law as complete as anybody I know of," he later wrote, "but I did it in my own room at Hiram."

In 1859 Garfield agreed to let Republican leaders nominate him for a seat in the Ohio state senate. He attended the state convention in August and was selected on the fourth ballot, or round of voting. He was part of the Republican ticket, but he rarely referred to the Republican Party in the forty or so two-hour speeches he gave on the campaign trail. Garfield beat his opponent 5,176 to 3,746 votes and became the senator from Summit and Portage counties.

Garfield entered politics at a critical time in the history of his country. On October 16, 1859, abolitionist leader John Brown and his men raided a federal arsenal, a storehouse for weapons, at Harpers Ferry in present-day West Virginia. They planned to distribute the arsenal's arms and ammunition to slaves in the South. The raiders' plot failed. John Brown was captured and sentenced to death.

John Brown (crouching, center right) *led a raid on the arsenal at Harpers Ferry (in modern West Virginia). The plot failed. Brown was arrested and hanged in 1859.*

———————————— ✧ ————————————

On December 2, the day Brown was hanged, Garfield made this entry in his journal: "A dark day for our country...I do not justify his acts...But I do accord to him...honesty of purpose and sincerity of heart." There would be many dark days ahead.

CHAPTER THREE

CIVIL WAR

*We can never hope for peace until we crush up
or disperse their [the South's] heavy armies and
remove the active cause of the sectional feud
[dispute between North and South].*
—James Garfield,
letter to friend Burke Hinsdale, September 12, 1862

In January 1860, James Garfield left Lucretia in Hiram and
went to Columbus, Ohio, to start his first term as state senator.
At twenty-eight, he was the youngest member of the legislature. Garfield knew little about the practical aspects of making
law, but he roomed with an experienced legislator, James Cox,
at the home of another senator. He learned quickly.

During his first session in the Ohio Senate, Garfield spoke
out against a proposed tax on dogs. He opposed the repeal of a
law providing for school libraries. And he argued that Ohio was
not responsible for the actions of John Brown and his raiders at
Harpers Ferry, even though they staged their attack from Ohio.

The Garfields welcomed the birth of their first child on July 3, 1860. Her name was Elizabeth Arabella, in honor of Garfield's mother. The next day, Garfield gave a speech in celebration of the Fourth of July. He proclaimed that "there were no men in America who would wish to break the Union."

But one month after Americans elected Abraham Lincoln president in November, South Carolina became the first state to secede, or break away, from the United States. Back in the Ohio Senate, Garfield wrote to his wife: "There is a strong warlike sentiment here. . . . I expect in a few days . . . I will be seen on the East portico [porch] of the State House learning the use of the light infantry musket [a type of gun]."

─────────────── ✧ ───────────────

A new Ohio capitol building was still under construction when Garfield won a seat in the state senate. The original capitol burned down in 1852. The new structure was finished in 1861.

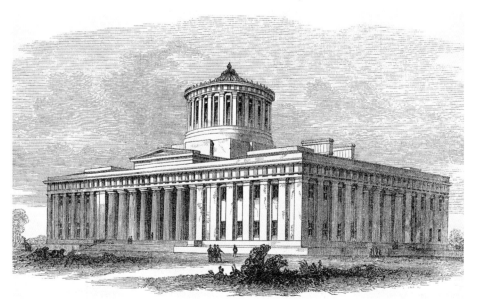

Mississippi, Florida, Alabama, and Georgia seceded in early January. And on January 26, 1861, the same day Garfield became a lawyer, Louisiana left the Union. Garfield favored harsh action against the Southern states and thought that president-elect Lincoln was a "firm, fearless man" who would abolish slavery and preserve the Union.

OFF TO WAR

In February 1861, the six seceding states and Texas formed the Confederate States of America and elected Jefferson Davis president. Shortly after taking office in March, Lincoln announced that he would send an unarmed supply ship to aid federal (U.S.) troops at Fort Sumter, South Carolina. On April 12, Confederate soldiers attacked the fort. The fort's defenders surrendered, Virginia joined the Confederacy, and the Civil War (1861–1865) began.

"The all absorbing and intense excitement which fills this city and state and whole nation has no parallel in our history," Garfield wrote from Columbus a few days later. "It has swept everything before it."

✧ ————————
The Civil War started in 1861 when Confederate troops fired on Fort Sumter in South Carolina.

Eventually, eleven states fought for the Confederacy. President Lincoln called upon states supporting the Union to provide seventy-five thousand soldiers to the cause. Ohio governor William Dennison asked Garfield to use his speaking skills to urge men to volunteer. Garfield read books on military science and studied battle maneuvers. At the end of April, he wrote to Lucretia: "The more I reflect on the whole subject, the more I feel that I cannot stand aloof from this conflict."

Garfield returned to Hiram to be with his wife and baby daughter. But in July, the governor appointed him lieutenant colonel in charge of the 42nd Ohio Volunteer Infantry Regiment. He left for Camp Chase, Ohio, in August and soon rose to the rank of colonel.

——————————— ✧ ———————————

Camp Chase, as shown in this Civil War era print, was laid out with military precision. It was located near Columbus, Ohio.

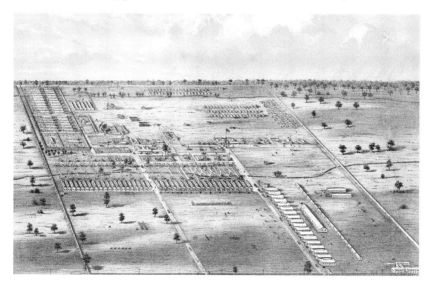

Garfield continued to recruit volunteers for Ohio's share of the Union army. By the end of November, the 42nd Ohio had about one thousand men, and on December 14, Garfield and his men boarded a train for eastern Kentucky. Their mission was to occupy an area along the Big Sandy River in Kentucky and, under the leadership of General Don Carlos Buell, to drive the Confederates from the state.

General Don Carlos Buell
——————— ✧ ———————

Garfield soon commanded the 18th Brigade, a group of about three thousand soldiers that included his regiment and three others—the 40th Ohio, 14th Kentucky, and 22nd Kentucky—plus some cavalry (soldiers on horseback). The brigade did not have any artillery (large guns) of its own. Garfield's job was to move ill-equipped and poorly trained troops over seventy-five miles of difficult road into the river valley, then to challenge Confederate forces under Brigadier General Humphrey Marshall. General Marshall, a graduate of the U.S. Military Academy at West Point, had served in the Mexican-American War (1846–1848). Garfield had virtually no military experience, but he did have specific instructions from General Buell.

By the brigade's first battle, exhaustion, disease, and desertion had reduced the number of Garfield's troops. The Confederates were dug in at Middle Creek, near Paintsville. Garfield made several mistakes about the location of the

Confederate forces. Several uncoordinated attacks and retreats took place that day—January 10, 1862. Both sides claimed victory, but during the night, the Confederates retreated to an area close to the Virginia border. Garfield's men had prevented the Confederates from moving into central Kentucky.

Garfield marched his men to Piketon (later called Pikeville), Kentucky, and awaited orders. A flood had polluted the water there, bringing dysentery and other diseases. Garfield contracted dysentery and battled with digestive problems from then on. More than fifty of his men died from their illnesses.

Garfield was promoted to brigadier general in March. He received orders to leave his troops and report to

————————— ✧
Brigadier General Garfield

General Buell in Tennessee. The general assigned him to the 20th Brigade, made up of two regiments from Ohio (the 64th and 65th), the 13th Michigan Regiment, and the 51st Indiana Regiment.

In April, Garfield and his men joined Union general Grant's forces at Pittsburg Landing, Tennessee, one day after the Battle of Shiloh—the fiercest of the fighting there. He wrote to Lucretia: "The horrible sights I have witnessed on this field, I can never describe. No blaze of glory that flashed around the magnificent triumphs of war can ever atone for the unwritten and unutterable horrors of the scene of carnage."

Garfield's brigade was part of the Union army's Sixth Division, which was in charge of building roads, digging trenches, and posting guards. Garfield supervised his troops as they repaired railroad lines. He was eager to pursue the Confederates camped in Corinth, Tennessee, but the Union army held back.

THE SOLDIER CONGRESSMAN

Meanwhile, Garfield's friends wrote letters encouraging him to seek the Republican Party's nomination for a seat in the U.S. House of Representatives. The district convention was scheduled for September 1862, only a few months away.

Garfield was impatient with his commanders and appalled to learn that the Union army did not protect slaves who escaped from their masters. He still suffered from dysentery and ate as little as possible to avoid a flare-up of the illness. But he wrote back to his friends that he would not resign from the army and actively campaign. On the other hand, he wouldn't refuse the nomination.

DISOBEYING ORDERS

While thirty-year-old James Garfield was in command of the 20th Brigade in the spring of 1862, a slave found his way to the Union camp and hid among the soldiers. His owner rode into camp and demanded that the division commander return the fugitive (runaway) slave. The commander ordered Garfield to tell his men to hunt down the slave.

Garfield refused. He wrote on the back of the commander's order: "I respectfully, but positively, decline to allow my command to search for, or deliver up, any fugitive slaves. I conceive that they are here for quite another purpose."

Disobeying a direct order usually meant a court-martial and severe punishment. When Garfield was told of this, he responded, "The matter may as well be tested first as last. Right is right. . . . My people on the Western Reserve of Ohio did not send my boys and myself down here for that kind of business, and they will back me up in my action."

Garfield was never charged with disobeying his superior officer. The War Department eventually issued a general order that the Union troops were not to turn over fugitive slaves to their former masters.

Garfield's health worsened. Unable to serve in the field, he was placed on a court-martial (military trial) panel. While waiting for decisive action against the Confederates, he spent his time listening to cases of misbehavior among the soldiers. He soon became so ill that on July 30 he was temporarily relieved of duty. Plagued by dysentery, discouraged and depressed, Garfield mounted his horse and started a weeklong, painful journey back to Hiram.

Garfield welcomed his time at home. He vacationed with Lucretia in Howland Springs, Ohio, to regain his health and escape the stresses of politics and war. The Republican convention met while he was away. After voting eight times for several candidates, the convention finally nominated him to run for Congress.

The election would not be until November. Rather than begin to campaign, Garfield traveled to Washington, D.C., in the middle of September. He felt better and hoped to return to active duty in the Union army.

On September 22, 1862, President Lincoln issued a proclamation that slaves within any state "in rebellion against the United States" as of January 1, 1863, would be considered free. Garfield wrote to Lucretia: "The President's proclamation gives great satisfaction among all strong vigorous men. . . . The President's heart is right. God grant he may have the strength to stand up to his convictions and carry them out to the full." The Emancipation Proclamation took effect on January 1, 1863, since none of the Confederate states had returned to the Union by then.

✧ ———————
Lincoln (third from left) *and his cabinet (advisers) discuss the Emancipation Proclamation.*

Garfield met with many political and military leaders while he was in the nation's capital. In November he was elected to the U.S. House of Representatives. But the session of Congress in which he would serve did not start until December 1863, more than a year away. In the meantime, Garfield was placed on another court-martial panel.

In January 1863, Garfield received a New Year's letter from an old friend, Burke A. Hinsdale. He wrote back, discussing the events of the past year. The two men started a correspondence that included a New Year's letter every year until Garfield's death.

After the courts-martial were over, Garfield received orders to join Major General William Rosencrans in Tennessee. He stopped to see his family in Hiram on his way to the new post. Garfield wanted to command troops, but instead, he became an adviser to Rosencrans. Garfield's main duties were to draft instructions and read reports. He and Rosencrans shared living quarters and enjoyed philosophical debates.

HERO AT CHICKAMAUGA

Restless and eager to attack Confederate forces, Garfield had to wait until August before Rosencrans ordered his troops forward. About eighty thousand Union soldiers headed for the Confederate position at Chattanooga, in what came to be called the Battle of Chickamauga.

Garfield was dissatisfied with the way in which the Chickamauga campaign was being fought by the Union army. He thought it was not attacking the Confederates boldly enough during about a month of skirmishes. He advised Rosencrans to leave the battle zone and go to

A journalist traveling with Union troops made this drawing of soldiers approaching Confederate forces in the Battle of Chickamauga in 1863. During the Civil War period, cameras were heavy and complicated to use. Few reporters had them.

headquarters at Chattanooga on September 20 to report on the battle. Meanwhile, Garfield stayed with General George Thomas to help defend the area. During the fighting, Garfield's horse was shot out from under him.

Garfield assisted General Rosecrans until October 10, when the general relieved him of duties so Garfield could travel to Washington, D.C., to start his term in Congress that December. The general's order read: "Brig. Gen. J. A. Garfield has been chosen by his fellow-citizens to represent them in the councils of the nation. His high intelligence, spotless integrity, business capacity and thorough acquaintance with the wants of the army will render his services more valuable if possible, to the country in Congress than with us."

Garfield returned from Tennessee to a house in Hiram that Lucretia had saved enough money to buy. She had also just given birth to their second child, Harry Augustus, on October 11. One day, in the parlor, Lucretia handed her husband a note. It stated that although they had been married for nearly five years, they had lived together less than twenty weeks. Garfield therefore resolved to bring "Crete," Elizabeth (whom he called "Trot"), and baby Harry with him to Washington while he served in Congress.

On December 1, just a few days before the first session of the 38th Congress began, Trot died after a sudden illness. She was three years old. Garfield wrote to a friend: "How desolate our hearts are tonight." Heartbroken but determined, Garfield went to Washington.

When Garfield arrived there, he was promoted to major general primarily because he returned to the Battle of Chickamauga after persuading General Rosecrans to leave for Chattanooga. Rosencrans was seen as abandoning his troops during battle and later lost his command. Garfield defended Rosecrans, but the warm friendship between the two men cooled.

Garfield was the elected representative from his district in Ohio. He consulted with President Lincoln about the conflict he felt between serving as a general or as a congressman. Lincoln told him that it was easier to find good generals than to find support for Republican causes in the U.S. House of Representatives. Garfield resigned from the army and, at thirty-two, became the youngest new representative in the House. But from then on, Lucretia often referred to her husband as "General Garfield."

LEGISLATING FOR VICTORY
Garfield found a desk in the noisy, crowded, dirty south wing of the Capitol building. Congressmen did not have offices then. They conducted their business from desks in

the House chamber, which was strewn with apple cores and other food scraps and stained with tobacco juice. Garfield was assigned to the House Military Affairs Committee, chaired by General Robert Schenck of Ohio.

The main business of this session of Congress was to supply and maintain the Union army. At the president's request, Garfield and other members of the committee wrote a bill to draft more men into the army. The bill passed in February 1864.

In March, General Ulysses S. Grant took command over all Union forces. Known as a tough leader, his command increased the likelihood that the Confederates would be defeated. On June 15, Garfield voted for the Thirteenth Amendment to the U.S. Constitution, which abolished slavery. When the congressional session ended on July 4, he returned to Ohio.

Abraham Lincoln won reelection in November 1864, and Garfield returned to Congress in December. This time he rented rooms near the Capitol for Lucretia and Harry.

Garfield soon earned a reputation as a good speaker. "The power of making a clear, compendious [brief] statement of a case is a most valuable one," he wrote. And he added that President Lincoln "was sometimes a model in that direction."

By this time, politicians were talking about the South's inevitable surrender. But Garfield thought that Lincoln's plans for ending the war and for the rebuilding of the war-torn South were too lenient. Others in Congress agreed with him. During that session (December 5, 1864, to March 3, 1865), Congress grew more and more divided about how to treat the Confederacy after the war. By the time Lincoln was sworn in for his second term as president on March 4, 1865, Garfield no longer supported Lincoln's Reconstruction (rebuilding) plans.

On April 9, 1865, Confederate general Robert E. Lee surrendered his forces to General Ulysses S. Grant at Appomattox Court House, Virginia. Five days later, President Lincoln was assassinated. According to Garfield campaign literature published many years later, Garfield was in New York City on April 17, 1865, when he came across a mob angered by Lincoln's assassination. He allegedly calmed the crowd by stepping forward and making a speech, which ended with: "Fellow citizens! God reigns and the government at Washington still lives." Garfield did not refer to the incident in his private papers, and possibly this is just an election campaign fable.

The Civil War officially ended on May 26, 1865. The former vice president, Andrew Johnson, who had become president after Lincoln's death, took over Reconstruction plans for the South. He initially ran the government primarily through executive orders, which don't need the approval of Congress.

The 38th Congress had adjourned (ended its session) in March, and Johnson did not convene (begin) the first session of the 39th Congress until December 4, 1865. In the meantime, Garfield continued his law practice and enjoyed his second son, James Rudolph, who had been born on October 17. He also studied hard to prepare himself for a leadership role in the House of Representatives. Soon it would be time for another election in Ohio, and he was determined to remain in Congress.

CHAPTER FOUR

RE-CREATING A NATION

As a result of the great growth of the country and of the new legislation arising from the late war, Congress is greatly overloaded with work.

—James Garfield,
Atlantic Monthly, July 1877

In the eight months since Lincoln's assassination, President Andrew Johnson—a Democrat from Tennessee—had acted on his own plans for the South. He allowed the Southern states to determine their own governments, without a role for African Americans. These governments established "black codes" that denied African Americans their rights and forced them to work for very low wages, often for their former masters.

When the first session of the 39th Congress began on December 4, 1865, the Republican leadership in the House and Senate refused to seat congressmen from the former Confederate states. The Republicans in Congress began to design their own Reconstruction policies for the South, policies in which African Americans would have a stronger role in government.

RADICAL RECONSTRUCTION

Moderate Republicans were willing to let President Johnson continue with most of his Reconstruction plans. James Garfield thought the president's plans did not fulfill all that the Union forces had fought for. He joined the Radical Republicans, whose leader in the House was Thaddeus Stevens from Pennsylvania. Stevens chaired the House Committee on Ways and Means, which holds great power over money for government services. He demanded that the federal government protect the civil rights of African Americans and Southern whites who had remained loyal to the Union.

Garfield strongly supported the abolition of slavery, which took effect when the Thirteenth Amendment to the Constitution was finally ratified (approved) by the states on December 18, 1865. That same month, a group of men met in Tennessee. They formed an organization— the Ku Klux Klan—to keep former slaves from claiming their rights.

In April 1866, Garfield voted for the Civil Rights Act, which gave additional rights to former slaves as citizens of the United States. President Johnson vetoed the bill, but Congress overrode his veto. In June, Congress proposed the Fourteenth Amendment to the Constitution, which gave African Americans citizenship and equal protection with whites under federal and state laws. Garfield insisted that former slaves should have the same right to vote as any other Americans, regardless of whether they could read or write.

He noted that if a state were going to create a literacy test for its citizens who wanted to vote, then that test ought to be given to every potential voter regardless of race. States would not be able to give the literacy test only to former slaves as a way to keep them from voting. The amendment also prohibited former officeholders who had supported the Confederacy from holding federal or state political office.

────────────── ✧ ──────────────

Ku Klux Klansmen disguised themselves when they terrorized former slaves. This etching, made from a photograph of arrested Klansmen, shows how some of them dressed.

Congress declared that none of the former Confederate states could be readmitted into the Union until they ratified the Fourteenth Amendment. President Johnson urged these states to reject the proposal. He felt that the treatment of freed slaves was a matter for each state to decide, not the national government. All of the states rejected the proposal, except Tennessee. On July 24, 1866, Tennessee became the first Confederate state to rejoin the Union.

The first session of the quarreling 39th Congress ended a few days later, and the second session did not start until December 3. During this break, Garfield studied books about finance, taxation, and tariffs (charges on imported goods). He wanted to lead the Committee on Ways and Means after Thaddeus Stevens, who was ill, retired.

In Garfield's congressional campaign that fall, he took a "hard money" position. During the war, the federal government had printed more paper money than it had in gold reserves. Garfield proposed that all paper money should be backed by gold in order to keep the value of the money from falling. He also called for import tariffs and other measures to protect U.S. industry from foreign competition. And he opposed the way large businesses forced smaller competitors out of business to create monopolies.

Garfield was elected from his Ohio district again and returned to Washington in December. To his disappointment, he was still assigned to the House Military Affairs Committee. His daughter Mary (nicknamed "Mollie") was born January 17, 1867. She joined brothers Harry, four, and James, two.

Garfield took up his children's cause in Congress. He wanted to establish a federal Department of Education,

In this Civil War era photograph, Garfield is seated in the center.

———————————— ✧ ————————————

under which a commissioner could gather information and help the states, state colleges, and the District of Columbia on education matters. Garfield's bill had been defeated in an earlier session of Congress. But in this session, Garfield was better known and more experienced. In introducing the bill, he said, "It is an interest that has no lobby to press its claims. It is the voice of the children of the land, asking us to give them all the blessings of civilization." The bill became law in 1867, and Henry Barnard was the first education commissioner.

The Republican-led Congress was in a state of total dis-agreement with President Johnson. Congress passed a series of laws, called the Reconstruction Acts, that divided the Confederate states—except for Tennessee—into five military districts, each run by federal troops. Johnson vetoed these laws, and Congress overrode his vetoes.

41st CONGRESS,
2d Session.

S. 359.

IN THE SENATE OF THE UNITED STATES.

DECEMBER 22, 1869.

Mr. Sumner asked, and by unanimous consent obtained, leave to bring in the fol-ing bill; which was read twice and ordered to be printed.

A BILL

To carry out the reconstruction acts in the State of Virginia, and to secure equality before the law.

Whereas in the act of Congress bearing date March two, eighteen hundred and sixty-seven, entitled "An act to provide for the more efficient government of the rebel States," among which was enumerated Virginia, it is provided, "that until the people of said rebel States shall be by law admitted to representation in the Congress of the United States, any civil government which may exist there shall be deemed provisional only, and in all respects subject to the paramount authority of the United States at any time to abolish, modify, control, or supersede the same," and such States are divided into military districts; and, whereas in the supplementary reconstruction act bear-ing date July nineteen, eighteen hundred and sixty-seven, it is further provided that "all persons hereafter elected or ap-pointed to office in said military districts under any so-called State or municipal authority shall be required to take and subscribe the oath of office prescribed by law for officers of the United States;" and whereas it was the true intent and meaning of the act aforementioned that persons allowed to participate in the provisional legislature of any

✧

This first page of Senate bill S. 359 is part of an 1869 bill that sought to establish the Reconstruction Acts in Virginia.

Congress also passed the Tenure of Office Act. It prevented a U.S. president from dismissing any federal officeholder confirmed by the Senate, unless the Senate gave its approval. This law was passed mainly because President Johnson wanted to remove Secretary of War Edwin Stanton, who was a Radical Republican. Again, Johnson vetoed the act. Again, Congress overrode his veto.

The 39th Congress officially ended on March 3, 1867. The 40th Congress started the next day. When Congress recessed in July, Garfield and Lucretia sailed for Europe. They visited England, Scotland, and Italy before returning home in October.

IMPEACHMENT

Meanwhile, President Johnson had asked Secretary of War Stanton to resign. Stanton refused. While Congress was out of session, Johnson suspended him and assigned Union general Ulysses S. Grant to take Stanton's place.

✧ ————————————

Edwin Stanton, secretary of war under Andrew Johnson, had a distinctive beard. It makes Stanton easy to spot in many photographs and etchings from this era. See page 40, for example.

In January 1868, Garfield was back in the House of Representatives when the Senate, citing the Tenure of Office Act, refused to accept Stanton's removal. President Johnson thought that the act was unconstitutional and that he had the right to dismiss a cabinet member. Johnson wanted to take the issue of presidential authority to the Supreme Court. Grant had resigned from the position, and in February Johnson appointed Lorenzo Thomas to be secretary of war in order to force a confrontation.

Congressional leaders saw their chance to remove a president whose Reconstruction plans for the South conflicted with theirs. First, the House drafted a resolution of impeachment against Johnson, charging him with "high crimes and misdemeanors in office." Among those voting for impeachment was Congressman Garfield.

Thaddeus Stevens delivers the last speech on impeachment before the House votes to try President Johnson in the Senate. An impeachment conviction in the Senate removes a president from office.

The House's impeachment resolution passed 126 to 47. On March 30, the Senate, which has the power to try a president on charges made by the House, began Johnson's impeachment trial. When the two-month trial ended, 35 senators voted guilty and 19 voted not guilty. Impeachment convictions need a two-thirds majority, and this was one vote shy. President Johnson stayed in office.

By then Garfield was considered an important leader among the Republicans in the House. In 1869 he became chairman of the Committee on Banking and Commerce. He fought for expanding federal census reports, which count the country's population every ten years. He wanted the reports to include economic and other information, but his idea wouldn't be adopted by Congress until almost a dozen years later. Garfield also voted for the proposed Fifteenth Amendment, which made it illegal to deny men the right to vote because of their race.

It looked as if Garfield might stay in Congress a while longer. He and Lucretia bought a three-story redbrick house in Washington. The family kept their smaller house in Hiram to, as Garfield put it, "roll on the grass there in the summer."

PRESIDENT GRANT

Although the Republicans failed to impeach Andrew Johnson, they did manage to elect Ohio Republican Ulysses S. Grant president in the next election. Grant was inaugurated on March 4, 1869. In his address to the nation, he asked for "patient forbearance [tolerance] one toward another . . . and a determined effort on the part of every citizen to do his share toward cementing a happy union."

This etching honoring passage of the Fifteenth Amendment illustrates
many of the rights the Constitution extended to
African Americans after the Civil War.

❖

About one year later, when the Fifteenth Amendment was
ratified by the states, all of the former Confederate states had
been readmitted to the United States. They had Republican-
controlled governments shaped by the Reconstruction Acts.
Hiram Revels, a Republican from Mississippi, became the
first African American U.S. senator. But the country was far
from a happy union. Quarrels over Reconstruction of the
South continued in Congress.

Thaddeus Stevens had died two months after Johnson's impeachment trial. Garfield still wanted Stevens's place as head of the Committee on Ways and Means, but House leadership gave the position to someone else. Even so, Garfield continued to work on financial matters. He helped to restore federal funds for education after a previous Congress gave no money to the Department of Education and reduced the department to a bureau within the Department of the Interior. He argued for spending government money on other educational and scientific projects, including the Smithsonian Institution (a national museum and research center) and the U.S. Naval Observatory, which studies astronomy. He joined the Board of Trustees of Hampton Institute, founded in 1868 to educate freed slaves.

When he wasn't working in Washington, Garfield enjoyed being with his family in Ohio. Another child was born on August 3, 1870. He was named Irvin McDowell, in honor of a Union general in the Civil War.

Garfield was disappointed with the Union general who had become president. Because Grant was a Republican from Ohio, Garfield felt obliged to support him. But the new president had little political experience. Grant appointed his friends and campaign contributors to government jobs regardless of whether they were qualified. He allowed them to take bribes and keep for themselves tariffs and other money that should have gone into the U.S. Treasury. Grant was not the first to allow these activities, but bribe-taking and other schemes to get money were particularly widespread in his administration.

Congress voted to take the first steps toward a more honest system, based on merit. It authorized the president to make rules for entering the government workforce, or civil service, and to appoint a commission to investigate how people got government jobs. Garfield was delighted. "I am exceedingly glad," he said, "that we are able at last to give, for the first time in the history of this Government, a legislative expression in favor of civil service reform."

Problems continued in the South. As Democrats there began to regain power, they found ways to prevent former slaves from voting or keeping office. Congress passed legislation that allowed federal officers to supervise elections, so that African Americans could continue to participate in state and local governments.

Congress had other problems to debate as well. They discussed ways to help the poor and to provide for the thousands upon thousands of people moving to the United States from Europe and Asia. They also argued over whether and how to prevent large, successful businesses from driving out their competition, especially in the railroad industry.

FIFTEEN-HOUR DAYS

In December 1871, Speaker of the House James Blaine appointed Garfield to chair the House Committee on Appropriations (spending). The committee is responsible for overseeing where the federal government spends every dollar, and Garfield took his job seriously. He worked closely with all of the federal departments, especially the Department of the Treasury, and inspected schools, hospitals, and office buildings. He wanted to find out what everything cost.

A major part of Garfield's job was to prepare about a dozen annual appropriations bills, which set forth how much each federal program could spend for the year. He worked hard. In April 1872, he wrote to a friend, "I am absolutely working fifteen hours a day and have been for the last three months and I am about as near used up as I ever was in my life."

Once all the appropriations bills became law, Garfield left for Montana. He enjoyed this first trip west of the Mississippi River. He rode with the drivers on the top of stagecoaches and slept under the stars in a buffalo robe.

Garfield had been sent as a U.S. commissioner to persuade the Native American Salish (Flathead) nation to move from the Bitter Root Reservation to another area provided for them by the federal government. The Salish didn't believe that the United States would honor its pledges of aid, since few promises the government made to the nation in an 1855 treaty had been kept. Garfield convinced them to move peacefully. He made a new treaty with the nation and helped to get them housing in their new location.

It seemed strange to Garfield that the federal government should draft treaties with Native Americans as if they were foreign nations. He doubted whether these treaties would ever be honored properly and thought that one solution would be to give full citizenship to Native American men.

But full citizenship was not what Garfield had in mind for women. He declined to support voting rights for women because "the suffrage [vote] is not the appropriate remedy for the many evils of which Woman so justly complains." He once wrote: "I cannot contemplate without horror that feature of the [women's rights] movement that tends to strike down the sanctity of marriage and break up the foundations of the family on which the purity, and peace and happiness of society depend."

Meanwhile, Lucretia Garfield stayed home with their growing family. Another child, Abram, was born on November 12, 1872. Managing the household while her husband was away, she once wrote about the "grinding misery of being a woman, between the [grinding labor] of household cares and training children."

GARFIELD FAMILY LIFE

His travels and work in Congress kept James Garfield away from his wife Lucretia for weeks and months at a time, particularly when their children were young. After their marriage in 1858, Lucretia gave birth to seven children between 1860 and 1874. Two died when they were toddlers.

Garfield adored playing with his children when he was home, but he realized that it was Lucretia who kept the family together. In a letter to her on May 20, 1880, after the older children were nearly grown, he put it this way, "I am sure you have never yet realized how entirely this family are centered on you and how every motion of your life is felt in the smallest fibre of every one of us. If I were to try I am sure I could not analyze the processes by which you have gained such an ascendency over us all, but the power is none the less real."

——————— ✧

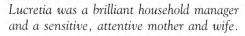

Lucretia was a brilliant household manager and a sensitive, attentive mother and wife.

SCANDAL

The 42nd Congress went into an unusual third session (a Congress usually has two sessions) from December 2, 1872, to March 3, 1873. Adding to tensions over Reconstruction policies in the South was a political scandal called the Crédit Mobilier affair.

In 1872 the *New York Sun* had published a story stating that Garfield and several others had taken bribes in 1867 and 1868 from Congressman Oakes Ames to approve a construction contract. Ames had connections with Crédit Mobilier, a corporation under contract to build the Union Pacific Railroad across the western United States. The *Sun* wrote that Ames gave stock in the corporation to Speaker of the House Blaine and to committee chairmen—including Garfield—in exchange for making sure that the corporation's business practices were not questioned.

Blaine formed a special committee to investigate these charges. The committee revealed that unethical deals by Crédit Mobilier had resulted in huge profits for the corporation's board of directors. Ames testified that he lent about three hundred dollars to Garfield, but that Garfield hadn't taken any stock in the company. Garfield testified that this was the case. But then Ames changed his testimony. He accused Garfield of asking him to put up three hundred dollars toward the purchase of one thousand dollars worth of stock. Ames also said that he had given Garfield ten shares of stock in 1868 and that Garfield never paid him.

Garfield did not defend himself publicly. Instead, he wrote to the judge on the committee explaining his innocence. About two weeks later, Ames told the committee: "Mr. Garfield understands this matter as a loan; he says I

In this political cartoon, the Crédit Mobilier scandal is the cake on the table. Uncle Sam (standing, left) scowls at figures who have taken pieces of the cake.

◇

did not explain it to him. . . . Mr. Garfield might have misunderstood me."

The committee recommended that Ames and another congressman be expelled from the House of Representatives, and they were. Ames died shortly afterward. However, the committee did not charge Garfield with any wrongdoing.

Garfield expected that the voters in Ohio would be angry over his role in the affair. To his surprise, as he wrote to Lucretia, "there is more agitation in regard to my vote on the increase of salaries of members of Congress than there is in regard to Crédit Mobilier." Garfield sent a letter to voters in his district in Ohio explaining that he had not been in favor of the salary increase either. He said that he had to accept the salary increase in order to get an appropriations bill passed.

RAILROADS

James Garfield and the U.S. railroad system shared an infancy. In 1830, a year before Garfield's birth, there were only three locomotives in the United States and 23 miles of track. Soon the railroad industry grew like crazy.

Victory in the Mexican-American War and California's 1849 gold rush spurred industrialists to expand the railroad system to link the United States from coast to coast. During Abraham Lincoln's presidency, the federal government agreed to lend money to two companies to build a railroad and a telegraph line linking Sacramento, California, and the Missouri River to the east. The Central Pacific Railroad imported thousands of Chinese workers to build the railroad east from California. The Union Pacific Railroad set out from Omaha, Nebraska, employing many Irish immigrants. The two lines met at Promontory, Utah, on May 10, 1869 *(below).* A telegrapher

tapped out a one-word message to President Grant in the White House: DONE. Celebrations sprang up across the country.

The race to build the railroads also resulted in illegal business deals such as the Crédit Mobilier scandal involving Representative Garfield and others in Congress. Tensions between railroad managers and their workers during the 1870s brought about the first general strike in the United States. Cattle drives to bring livestock to the trains made the cowboy era famous. Railroads also crossed through many Native American hunting grounds along the Great Plains, heightening tensions between Native Americans and white settlers.

During Garfield's lifetime, about 100,000 miles of track crisscrossed the country. Railroads had become a key part of the nation's economy and transportation system.

Garfield wrote his annual New Year's letter to his friend Burke Hinsdale. In it, he summed up 1873 this way: "To me the last year has been the stormiest of my life."

LEAVING PUBLIC SERVICE?

Despite some newspaper editorials questioning his actions with Crédit Mobilier, Garfield continued to chair the Committee on Appropriations when the 43th Congress met. With elections in southern states increasingly going to the Democrats, Garfield's Republican Party was only barely in control of the House. "I have never known the House in so disagreeable a temper," he wrote.

Garfield recognized that changes had to be made in the government's policy on money and commerce. Toward the end of 1873, the stock market fell sharply as people bought shares of railroad and other companies, without really having the money to pay for these investments. Companies went bankrupt, and thousands of people lost their jobs. The country plummeted into an economic depression.

Garfield pushed for reforms to curb inflation (rising prices). He was angered when other members of Congress wanted to pass a bill to print more dollars than were backed by reserves of gold. He argued that enough money was already in circulation. Speaking on the House floor, he called the bill a "path to disaster and disgrace." Congress passed the bill anyway, but Garfield convinced President Grant to veto it.

Garfield won the congressional election from his district in 1874, but he was no longer enthusiastic about returning to his seat in Congress. Another son, Edward, was born on Christmas Day. Garfield liked life at home and decided to

James A. Garfield in the 1870s
——————————— ◇

change careers. He had
become a lawyer in 1861
and had argued several cases
since then. He felt ready to
take on a legal practice full-time.

In his 1875 New Year's letter to Hinsdale, Garfield
wrote: "I want to feel free once again to do some work for
myself. Fifteen years ago today I took the oath of Office as
State Senator and I have not been an hour out of public
service since then."

CHAPTER FIVE

DARK HORSE

Now more than ever the people are responsible
for the character of their Congress. If that
body be ignorant, reckless, and corrupt, it is
because the people tolerate ignorance,
recklessness, and corruption.

—James Garfield,
Atlantic Monthly, July 1877

Since Garfield's 1875 New Year's letter to Burke Hinsdale, tensions in Congress and between Congress and the Grant administration had become even worse. As federal troops tried in vain to keep order in the South, Democrats there continued to destroy the state governments that were reorganized during Reconstruction.

On March 1, 1875, Radical Republicans in Congress enacted a civil rights bill. The act stated: "All persons within the jurisdiction of [legal system of] the United States shall be entitled to the full and equal enjoyment of the accommodations, advantages, facilities, and privileges of inns, public conveyances [transport] on land or water, theaters, and other places of public amusement . . . regardless of any previous condition of servitude."

Garfield sided with more moderate Republicans and voted against the measure. He thought that although the Constitution guaranteed political rights, such as the right of African Americans to vote, the Constitution did not provide for social equality. The Supreme Court later agreed and struck down the law.

After Congress adjourned in March 1875, Garfield took a vacation from the appropriations bills. He traveled to California while Lucretia and their children stayed in Ohio. During the two months that he was away, Garfield sent letters home. He included lessons in geography and history for the children and made up puzzles for the two older boys, Harry and James, to solve. Garfield had severe intestinal problems on the trip and recuperated when he got home.

"IT MUST BE DONE"

While Garfield was away, President Grant and his administration were at the center of another scandal. This time whiskey distillers and federal officers had siphoned off (stolen) money from the taxes collected on whiskey and used it to get rich and to bribe other government officials. Garfield no longer supported Grant and did not want him to run for a third term as president. Still wanting to leave politics, he wrote in his journal: "I shrink from starting out into a new career but it must be done." Garfield hoped to enter a law firm and move his family to Cleveland.

In the meantime, Garfield had dutifully taken his seat in the first session of the 44th Congress, which started December 6, 1875. Although the Republicans still held the Senate and the White House, Democrats had won the majority in the House of Representatives. The majority party usually appoints its own members to lead committees, so Garfield no longer chaired the Committee on Appropriations. Instead, he became a member of the House Committee on Ways and Means—finally! But by this time, his party was in the minority in the House, and he was able to accomplish very little.

The Republicans decided to nominate Rutherford B. Hayes, then the governor of Ohio, as their candidate for president. Garfield's Ohio friends urged him to stay on in politics and perhaps gain a more influential position if Hayes won. At about the same time, Garfield couldn't get the terms he wanted in a negotiation with a law firm. So in July 1876, he announced that he would once again run for Congress.

HELPING HAYES

That summer and fall, Garfield campaigned for himself and for Hayes. It was a three-way race for both men. New York governor Samuel Tilden ran as the Democrats' presidential candidate. New York industrialist Peter Cooper was the presidential nominee of the Greenback Party. Garfield's congressional seat from Ohio was challenged by both a Democrat and a Greenbacker.

The Greenback Party had formed shortly after financial markets collapsed in 1873 and many farmers fell deep in debt. The party proposed to increase the amount of paper money (greenbacks) in circulation as a way to boost prices

*In a newspaper from 1873, drawings showing mobs of investors
trying to enter closed financial institutions illustrate
a story about the financial panic that year.*

on farm products. Garfield, who wanted paper money to
be strictly tied to the amount of gold the government had
in reserve, thought Greenbacker proposals would only make
the economy worse.

Garfield's Greenbacker opponent was G. N. Tuttle of Painesville. During the campaigning, Garfield bought a farm near Painesville, in Mentor. Although he had tried often to leave his mother's farm when he was a boy, he wrote that he wanted a farm where "my boys can learn to work, and where I . . . can touch the earth and get some strength from it."

Edward, not quite two, did not live to see the farm. While on a campaign trip in New Jersey, Garfield received a telegram that his young son was gravely ill with whooping

————————————— ◇ —————————————

In modern times, the Garfield family's big farmhouse in Mentor, Ohio, is the James A. Garfield National Historic Site (below).

cough. Garfield rushed home. Shortly afterward, on October 25, 1876, Edward died. James and Lucretia buried Edward on Hiram Hill, next to Trot, their first child.

Garfield easily defeated Tuttle and the Democratic Party candidate on election day, November 7. The Greenback Party received only 81,737 votes for Cooper in the national election. But the presidential winner was far from certain.

The popular vote turned out this way:

Samuel J. Tilden (Democrat)	4,284,020
Rutherford B. Hayes (Republican)	4,036,572
Peter Cooper (Greenback)	81,737

But the winner in presidential elections is the person who receives a majority of the electoral votes. In this case, a majority would have been at least 185 of the 369 electoral votes. Tilden had 184. Hayes had at least 165 votes. This left 20 votes in dispute.

The Democrats and Republicans accused each other of unfairly interfering with voting in Florida, Louisiana, Oregon, and South Carolina. On November 10, President Grant asked Garfield to oversee the recounting of Louisiana's votes.

Garfield didn't want to go. He wrote to Hinsdale the next day, wondering "what shall be done to secure an honest and faithful count of the votes actually cast?"

President Grant persisted, and Garfield went to New Orleans. He stayed for two weeks, examining ballots and speaking with election officials. At the end of that time, he reported that Louisiana had properly cast its electoral votes for Hayes. The Democrats challenged his findings.

Congress prepared to count electoral votes. Florida, Louisiana, South Carolina, and Oregon each submitted two sets of electors—one favoring Tilden and the other favoring Hayes.

The Electoral College

The Constitution requires U.S. presidents and vice presidents to be elected by the electoral college—a group of people selected by each state and the District of Columbia. On election day, we really vote for these electors and not the candidates!

Each state has the same number of electors as it has senators and representatives in Congress. Washington, D.C., has three electors. The electors are usually picked by the political parties in the state. Each elector casts two votes—one for president and one for vice president. Electors in many states are pledged (promised) to vote for the candidate who wins most of the popular vote (one vote more than half) in that state. This is called "winner take all." Maine and Nebraska don't have a winner-take-all method. They allow electoral votes to be split among the candidates. Electors in some states are not required to vote for the candidate they pledged to support, but they almost always do.

After the vote in their state, the electors make a list of the number of votes each candidate received. They sign the list and certify that it is true, then send the list to the U.S. Senate. Copies of the list go elsewhere for safekeeping. The president of the Senate reads the list of electoral votes for president and vice president from each state.

Each candidate has to get a majority of the electoral votes to win. In the early twenty-first century, the number of electoral votes is 538 (100 senators, 435 representatives, and 3 for the District of Columbia), so the majority needed to win is 270.

If a candidate receives a majority, the president of the Senate announces the winner. If nobody has a majority of electoral votes, the House of Representatives selects a president from the top three candidates. Each state casts one vote. The Senate selects the vice president the same way from the top two candidates.

Because of the winner-take-all method, it is possible for a candidate for whom most people voted nationwide to lose to a candidate who received more electoral votes. That happened in the elections of 1824, 1876, 1888 and, in modern times, with the Bush-Gore election of 2000.

Garfield served on the special commission that decided the outcome of the U.S. presidential election of 1880.

Since the Constitution doesn't provide a way to resolve disputed electoral votes, Congress created a special fifteen-person commission (eight Republicans and seven Democrats) to decide the election.

Garfield believed that Congress did not have the authority to investigate the electoral voting procedures in the states. But nonetheless, he found himself appointed to the very commission he thought was unconstitutional. In meeting after meeting with business leaders, politicians, and others, he helped to negotiate what became known as the Compromise of 1877. The commission decided that Hayes was the winner, with 185 electoral votes to Tilden's 184.

In return for allowing the election to go to Hayes, Democrats wanted Hayes to withdraw the last of the federal occupying forces in the South and to appoint southern Democrats to government positions. Soon after taking office, Hayes removed the remaining federal troops from Louisiana and elsewhere. He appointed Senator David Key, a Democrat from Tennessee, to be postmaster general.

With federal troops gone, the Reconstruction era in the South was over. African Americans who had gained leadership positions were driven from office. Conditions worsened for former slaves and any others who had dared to support equal rights for them in southern society.

TROUBLED TIMES

House members, including Garfield, passed bills that would have ended the most harmful practices of corporate tycoons, the business leaders who controlled more and more of the United States' growing industries. But the Senate had refused to enact these bills into law. As these rich businessmen controlled larger and larger parts of their industries, they wiped out smaller businesses and laid off workers. The economic depression deepened.

During the summer of 1877, many poor working people living in squalid conditions in crowded cities drank polluted water, sickened, and died. In the first week of July, the *New York Times* wrote, "Already the cry of the dying children begins to be heard. . . . Soon, to judge from the past, there will be a thousand deaths of infants per week in the city." Tensions between employers and their workers erupted into large-scale violence.

On July 16, railroad workers in Martinsburg, West Virginia, walked off the job and shut down operations there when the Baltimore & Ohio Railroad announced a 10 percent cut in wages, the second cut in eight months. The strike spread until about one hundred thousand workers were on strike and more than half of the nation's rail freight traffic ground to a halt.

During a congressional debate about how much money to appropriate to the army, Garfield waved a stack of telegrams he declared governors had sent asking for federal troops. Garfield argued that fifty thousand soldiers were needed to protect Americans from the "red fool-fury of the

Striking Baltimore & Ohio Railroad workers drag the engineers off a train in Martinsburg, West Virginia, on July 17, 1877.

Seine [a river in Paris] transplanted here, taking root in our disasters." Seven years earlier, a popular revolution had overthrown Emperor Napoleon III in France. Fearing a similar action in the United States, President Hayes surrounded Washington, D.C., with federal troops.

Emperor Napoleon III

———— ✧ ————

Garfield supported the right to strike but was opposed to workers pressuring other workers to strike as well. He thought that businesses shouldn't unite with businesses against labor, and labor shouldn't form unions to fight against businesses. Both these actions, he argued, threatened the well-being of the nation.

By this time, Garfield had become minority leader in the House. His main job was to work for the interests of the Republicans in Congress and to support President Hayes. In 1878 the Greenbackers had joined with labor groups to become the Greenback-Labor Party, and their candidates won fourteen seats in the House. Part of Garfield's job as minority leader was to prevent these new members of Congress from voting with the Democrats and to undercut the Democrats as much as possible.

Garfield was not much of a political fighter. He preferred to study an issue and vote on its merits. He wanted to persuade people to vote his way by reasoning with them rather than making deals. His journal for February 25, 1879, notes: "I think there is a danger that I am getting too spiritless in regard to personalities but the fact is, I thoroughly despise all mere personal debates. I never feel that to slap a man in the face is any real gain to the truth."

A good book and stimulating conversation over dinner were more to Garfield's liking than political fighting in Congress. He adopted a stray dog and played with him and the children. He also enjoyed going to concerts and the theater. In 1879 alone, he saw Gilbert and Sullivan's *H.M.S. Pinafore* four times!

SENATOR-ELECT

When Congress met in March 1879, Garfield was again House minority leader. His most noted accomplishment during that session was a minor but important provision stuck in the midst of an appropriations bill. That provision established the U.S. Geological Survey for "classification of the public lands,

The CAPTAIN and SWEET LITTLE BUTTERCUP.
BUTTERCUP: "How sweetly he carols forth his melody to the unconscious moon."

H.M.S. PINAFORE

❖ ————————————

A poster advertising an 1879 production of H.M.S. Pinafore and examination" of the geology, mineral resources, and products of the nation.

By the summer of 1879, Garfield's friends began to pressure him to run for governor of Ohio or a seat in the Senate. He focused instead on matters at home. Sons James and Harry had been tutored by a governess for the past two years because Garfield thought they hadn't done well in school. He decided to send them to Saint Paul's Academy in Concord, New Hampshire.

Finally making up his mind in October, Garfield wrote in his journal: "If I were to act on my own choice . . . I would remain in the House. . . . But I have resolved to be a candidate for the U.S. Senate." He listed these reasons: (1) he would be "likely to break down" under stresses as minority leader; (2) there were good men in his district who wanted to be a representative; and (3) a refusal to run would play into the hands of those who thought he was afraid "to risk my strength in the larger field of the Senate."

So Garfield let it be known that he was interested in a Senate seat, then he and Lucretia set about enlarging their farmhouse in Mentor, Ohio. Since U.S. senators were elected by state legislatures then, Garfield did very little campaigning. His rivals for the Senate withdrew, and he was formally elected without opposition on January 13, 1880. By then senator-elect Garfield was back in the House serving as minority leader.

Garfield expected to serve in the House until March of 1881—the end of the 46th Congress. In fact, his last day there was May 25, 1880. A few days later, he left for the Republican National Convention in Chicago, Illinois.

James Blaine, a U.S. senator representing Maine, was a powerful figure at the 1880 Republican National Convention. He led a group that strongly opposed a third term for President Grant.
✧ ——————————

DARK HORSE

Almost fifteen thousand delegates to the convention crowded into the Glass Palace, a new exposition hall built after the great Chicago Fire of 1871 had destroyed much of the city. The Republicans were deeply divided between the "Stalwarts"—those who supported former president Grant for a third term as president—and those who were dead set against Grant's nomination. New York senator Roscoe Conkling, undisputed leader of his state's political party, controlled the Stalwarts. His rival was Maine senator James Blaine, a former Speaker of the House and powerful rival.

In a letter home, Garfield wrote: "No definite things appear on the face of this chaos. . . . I would gladly exchange this turmoil for the smaller and sweeter turmoil of the farm." Lucretia wrote back, describing the renovations to the farm, and added: "I hope you find the situation no worse than you expected—on the contrary, better. . . . Ever your own—Crete."

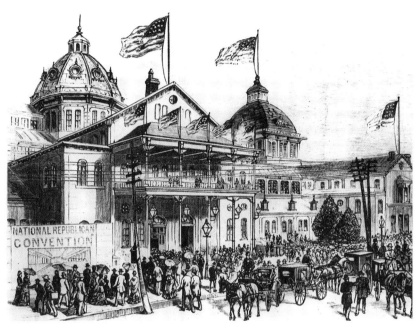

*Crowds gather for the 1880 Republican National Convention
at Chicago's Glass Palace.*

Garfield led the Ohio delegation. He avoided taking sides by nominating Ohio's secretary of the treasury John Sherman. After the first ballot on June 7, Blaine received 284 votes and Grant received 304. A candidate needed 379 to win.

On the second ballot, a Pennsylvania delegate gave one vote to James Garfield. No one seemed to take that vote seriously. But about twenty-four hours and thirty-three ballots later, when the Wisconsin delegation suddenly cast sixteen votes for James Garfield, the audience cheered. Garfield suddenly looked like the man who might be the compromise candidate. He was the "dark horse" of the convention—the person who unexpectedly wins a race.

With Blaine's consent, his people threw their support behind Garfield. Having gotten an agreement that a New Yorker would be nominated as vice president, Conkling changed enough votes for Garfield to win on ballot 36.

Chester A. Arthur, president of New York's Republican Central Committee, won the nomination even though many thought he was not qualified. But as one commentator noted at the time, "[T]here is no place in which the powers of mischief will be so small as in the vice presidency. . . . [I]t is true General Garfield, if elected, may die during his term of office, but this is too unlikely a contingency to be worth making extraordinary provision for."

Garfield made his way home by train, with crowds cheering him along the way. He stopped to make a commencement speech at Hiram College, where his close friend, Burke Hinsdale, was president. Then the next day, he and Lucretia stood in the Mentor train station to greet neighbors.

Lawnfield—a name reporters gave to the Mentor farm—became the site of Garfield's "front-porch campaign." When groups of visitors arrived, he gave a short speech and served refreshments. Garfield's supporters fought

✧ ———————————

Many visitors crossed Lawnfield's front porch during the 1880 presidential campaign. Garfield (facing page) won the election.

most of the hard political battles, while Garfield stayed out of the fight. That was considered appropriate for major presidential candidates then.

The Democrats nominated General Winfield Scott Hancock. The Greenbackers nominated James Weaver as their candidate. He campaigned for what was then considered to be radical notions: the right of women to vote in federal elections, taxes on a person's income that required the rich to pay a higher percentage than the poor, and federal regulation of trade among the states. The Prohibition Party, hoping to stop the sale of alchoholic beverages nationwide, nominated Neal Dow.

The popular vote in November 1880 showed an even closer contest than between Hayes and Tilden four years earlier. Garfield received about 4,450,000 popular votes and Hancock 4,440,000. Weaver received 308,578 and Dow received 10,305.

As Garfield knew, it's the electoral vote that matters. And here Garfield, who needed 185, won easily 214 to 155. He gained the electoral votes in Indiana and New York, thanks to a few thousand votes there. Conkling had worked hard to deliver New York voters. Garfield's election was not challenged.

Inventor Thomas Edison hung a string of his improved electric lights in front of his house on the night before the election and told an assistant: "If Garfield is elected, light up that circuit." He did.

When Garfield (standing right) was sworn in as the twentieth president of the United States in 1881, his mother Eliza (seated far left, front) was there. She was the first mother of a president to attend an inauguration.

CHAPTER SIX

LASTING LEGACIES

And now, fellow-citizens, I am about to assume the great trust which you have committed to my hands. I appeal to you for that earnest and thoughtful support which makes this Government in fact, as it is in law, a government of the people.
—James Garfield,
inaugural address, March 4, 1881

Inauguration Day—March 4, 1881—was bitterly cold. Snow covered the U.S. Capitol grounds. Many people stayed away from the swearing in of the nation's twentieth president, but not eighty-year-old Eliza Garfield. She became the first mother of a president to attend her son's inauguration.

Addressing the nation's fifty-one million or so fellow citizens, Garfield said, "The elevation of the negro race from slavery to the full rights of citizenship is the most important political change we have known since the adoption of the Constitution of 1787. . . . It has surrendered to their own guardianship the manhood of more than 5,000,000 people, and has opened to each one of them a career of freedom and usefulness."

An invasion of office seekers had pursued James Garfield from the moment he was elected. So he noted in his inaugural speech: "The civil service can never be placed on a satisfactory basis until it is regulated by law." The civil service reforms passed several years earlier were virtually useless, since Congress had stopped funding the program.

Garfield made sure that qualified African Americans received government jobs in his administration. He and his cabinet picked many of the people filling more than 100,000 federal positions.

In his first week in the White House, Garfield met hundreds of men who wanted jobs, and he soon tired of what he thought was a troublesome task. He wrote in his journal: "I must resist a very strong tendency to be dejected and unhappy at the prospect which is offered by the work before me."

During that first week, a thin young man named Charles Guiteau met with Garfield and showed him a speech—"Garfield against Hancock"—that Guiteau had circulated during the campaign. Guiteau wrote "Paris consulship" (a diplomatic position representing the United States in France) on the front cover. He watched Garfield start to read the speech and, satisfied that the president would appoint him to the position, he quietly left.

Thousands of guests came to the White House in the first week after the inauguration. At a White House reception,

The assassination of Czar Alexander II of Russia (right) on March 13, 1881, seemed to have little to do with Garfield's presidency.
——————— ✧

Guiteau introduced himself to the First Lady, shook her hand, and gave her his business card. Then he pronounced his name for her—"GET-oh."

On March 13, Czar Alexander II of Russia was shot and killed. Other European leaders had been assassinated in recent years, but Garfield decided not to have soldiers posted at the White House gates. He said, "Assassination can no more be guarded against than death by lightning; and it is best not to worry about either."

Garfield chose Joseph Stanley Brown as his private secretary and a staff of seven clerks to handle all the mail, visitors, and government callers. Garfield paid for them—as well as for meals and entertaining White House guests—out of his own annual salary of fifty thousand dollars.

Members of his cabinet came from both sides of the Republican Party. Cabinet members included William Windom (secretary of the treasury), Samuel Kirkwood (secretary of the interior), Wayne MacVeagh (attorney general), Thomas James (postmaster general), William Hunt (secretary of the navy), and Robert Todd Lincoln (secretary of war). Secretary of state, a higly influential position, went to James Blaine.

Under the Constitution, the Senate has the authority to approve presidential appointments. Tensions over Blaine's appointment mounted between President Garfield and Senator Roscoe Conkling, the powerful Stalwart leader. Conkling grudgingly allowed the Senate to accept Blaine's appointment. But on March 23, Garfield presented another list of appointments that Conkling was not about to tolerate.

✧ ————————

Robert Todd Lincoln, Garfield's secretary of war, was President Abraham Lincoln's son.

On the list to be collector for the Port of New York was William Robertson—who was loyal to Blaine. The powerful post involved receiving all tariffs on imported goods coming into the United States through New York City. Conkling wanted the current Stalwart collector to remain in the post.

In early April, senators formed a committee to forge an agreement between Garfield and Conkling. Garfield met with the committee and laid out his case. He said that it wasn't fair to him that the senators were afraid to confront Conkling. The president ought to have more flexibility to carry out his programs with men he trusted.

Other work with Congress went much more smoothly. At Garfield's request, Clara Barton (a prominent nurse) met with Secretary of State Blaine in April to talk about the Red Cross. Barton wanted the United States to sign the Geneva Convention, which established the Red Cross as an international aid organization. This required Congress's approval,

Clara Barton

———————— ✧ ————————

and Blaine agreed to help. Barton established the National Association of the Red Cross in the United States. She asked Garfield to lead the organization, but he nominated her instead.

Meanwhile, Garfield had learned of complaints that certain mail delivery routes—called Star Routes—were being operated dishonestly. Garfield asked the postmaster general

to investigate and learned that the government had contracted with private companies to deliver the mail to
9,225 routes in remote areas. These companies over-
charged the government for their services. Some routes
didn't even exist.

The Star Route fraud had operated during the Hayes
administration but had been ignored. Garfield was not
about to do the same. During the middle of April, he
fired those in government who were responsible or
allowed them to resign.

Even during the first hectic weeks at the White House,
Garfield found some time to relax. Books seemed to be
everywhere. Garfield continued to keep a catalog, which
he had started in 1872, of every book he read. He also
played billiards in the room President Grant had designed
for that purpose and went horseback riding along the
Potomac River.

While James and Harry studied for their entrance examination for Williams College, the younger Garfield children
enjoyed life at the White House. Abram, eight, raced bicy-
cles with his brother Irvin across the vast carpeting of the
East Room. Irvin, ten, rode his bicycle down the marble
staircase, frightening the White House staff. Mary, fourteen,
played the grand piano.

As was expected of a first lady, Lucretia Garfield
received guests at the White House twice a week. She and
the president hosted formal parties and occasionally enjoyed
a private dinner with old friends. After one such dinner in
April, Garfield wrote: "We gave a . . . very pleasant party
and good dinner *sine vino* [without wine]. . . . A welcome
relief from politics and offices!"

Garfield's children all appear in this photograph taken in 1881. Shown are (from left to right) Mary ("Mollie"), Harry, James, Irvin, and Abram.

In early May, while senators remained deadlocked over whether to appoint Robertson to be collector for the Port of New York, Lucretia suddenly fell ill. The White House was dangerously near a swamp of the polluted Potomac River, and the first lady's doctors guessed she had malaria or typhoid fever. Distraught, as she lay near death, Garfield stayed by her side as much as possible, sleeping only a few hours a night.

The Senate battle continued. Tom Platt, the junior senator from New York, was stuck in the middle. He didn't want to go against Conkling, the senior senator from New York, by voting for Robertson, whom Garfield had appointed. As a Republican, he didn't want to go against Garfield and block Robertson's nomination. So Platt convinced Conkling to try a face-saving maneuver.

On May 16, both senators resigned their seats and left for New York. They planned to stay away long enough for the remaining senators to confirm Robertson's appointment, then return to the Senate after the New York legislature reelected them.

Shortly after Conkling and Platt left, the Senate voted unanimously to approve Robertson's appointment. Then Robertson led a successful fight in the New York legislature to oppose reelection of Conkling and Platt. Their plan to return to the Senate had backfired.

✧ ————————
Roscoe Conkling had represented New York in the U.S. Senate since 1867. He resigned in 1881.

At the end of May, Lucretia started to recover. A week or so later, she and the family watched John Philip Sousa lead the Marine Band in a concert on the White House lawn. Then the president, the first lady, Abram, Irvin, and Mary took the train to a hotel in Elberon, New Jersey, just south of the fashionable seaside resort of Long Branch. Except for an awkward moment when Garfield met former president Grant, who was vacationing nearby, he enjoyed himself thoroughly. Abram and Irvin later took a train to Ohio to spend the summer with their grandmother and other relatives.

On June 27, Garfield returned to Washington to prepare for a long summer vacation starting on July 2. Congress had adjourned. Secretary of State Blaine and the president met and talked about U.S. foreign relations policies to be discussed with Congress in the fall. They also talked about a peace conference of all Western Hemisphere nations to be held in Washington in March 1882.

Garfield, his wife, and the older children expected to travel most of the summer and to see Irvin, Abram, and relatives in Ohio. Garfield planned to attend the twenty-fifth anniversary of his graduation from Williams College and to enroll Harry and James there for the fall term. Early on the morning of July 2, he strode into Harry's bedroom singing. Harry did a handstand on his bed and challenged his father to do the same. Garfield did.

Garfield shook hands with the domestic staff at the White House and left with James Blaine for the railroad station near the Capitol. The two men, plus Harry and James, who came in another carriage, were taking the train to Philadelphia, Pennsylvania, where they would meet Lucretia and Mary on their way back from Elberon.

Other members of Garfield's cabinet were already on the train when he and Blaine arrived.

As Garfield walked through the waiting room toward the train, Charles Guiteau took aim with an ivory-handled, .44-caliber, five-shooter English Bulldog pistol that he had recently bought and learned to shoot. He fired two shots. The first grazed the president's right arm. The second hit him squarely in the back.

Garfield fell forward, and Guiteau ran toward the exit. A janitor ran for a doctor, while a waiting room attendant rushed to help the president. Two policemen caught Guiteau. Harry and James, who had just arrived, knelt by their father's side.

In the commotion, Guiteau was heard to shout: "I am a Stalwart and Arthur will be President!" Garfield was heard to whisper to Smith Townshend, a city health officer who rushed to the scene, "Doctor, I am a dead man."

Secretary of War Robert Todd Lincoln sent for Dr. D. W. Bliss immediately after the shooting. Bliss took charge of Garfield's case.

Garfield was carried back to the White House and given morphine. He endured examinations from a host of doctors. Blaine's wife, Harriet, stayed with him until Lucretia, who had received a telegram in Elberon, arrived by a special train that nearly derailed before arriving in Washington, D.C.

Vice President Chester A. Arthur, who was in New York City consulting with Roscoe Conkling, came to the White House the next day. He wasn't allowed to see Garfield. Shaken but hopeful that the president would recover, Arthur told the cabinet members gathered there: "God knows I do not want the place I was never elected to."

In the first forty-eight hours, Bliss and at least a dozen other doctors examined Garfield, often sticking their fingers or metal probes into the wound in his back. They couldn't agree on where exactly the bullet was or how to treat the president's injury.

The use of x-rays to show metal objects had not yet been discovered. In late July, Alexander Graham Bell and Simon Newcomb tried their new metal-detecting device. Newcomb had noticed that electrically charged wire coil hummed when near metal. Bell used the telephone apparatus to amplify the humming sound. The device produced a hum no matter where they placed it near the president. Puzzled, the two men retested the device in the laboratory

◇ ─────────────

Inventor Alexander Graham Bell (left) used telephone technology that he had perfected in the metal-detecting device that he and Simon Newcomb tried to use to find the bullet in Garfield's body.

and returned to the White House. The problem was still the same. Garfield was lying on a new kind of mattress that had metal springs inside. Bell and Newcomb didn't know that. Had the president been placed on the floor, the device would likely have worked.

Medical disputes among Garfield's doctors leaked into the newspapers despite denials by Dr. Bliss. He and others also lied to reporters about the president's condition, later claiming that they didn't want Garfield to read bad news about himself. They rarely allowed him to read newspapers, although he did learn in late July that the New York legislature had elected two new senators to replace Platt and Conkling. On August 1, Robertson took his post as Port of New York collector.

Since the White House backyard was a swamp, doctors gave Garfield quinine to reduce the chances of getting mosquito-borne malaria. In spite of this treatment, he may have contracted malaria anyway.

The summer heat was stifling in Washington. Several schemes were devised to keep the president's room relatively cool and less humid. Most of them, such as wetting the curtains with ice water, did little good. Navy engineers set up a device in the basement that forced air through ice and thin cotton screens up into vents in Garfield's room. This simple air conditioner would have helped if the doctors hadn't insisted on keeping the windows open.

The president lay on his back day after day, eating little, wracked by fevers and chills, oozing blood and then pus, as infections set in. Blood poisoning paralyzed the right side of his face. The doctors gave him nourishment rectally, but still he slowly starved. By late August, the formerly robust president was down to 130 pounds.

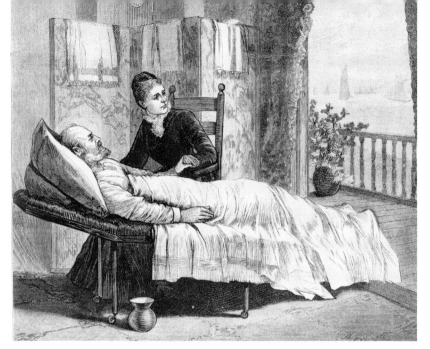

Garfield's health improved briefly at the seashore.

The government did little during the summer. Secretary of State Blaine and Garfield's private secretary, Joseph Stanley Brown, muddled through. Vice President Arthur returned to New York and waited.

In September Garfield demanded to go to the seashore again. The railroad provided him a special car. One group of men built a short line from the depot to the main track, while others worked through the night to lay 3,200 feet of track from the train station in Elberon to a cottage near the beach. The president made his trip on September 6, with thousands of people lining the route.

Garfield had his bed placed where he could see the ocean. Once or twice he even reclined in a chair by a window. "This is delightful," he told his doctors. "It is such a change."

The improvement in Garfield's health didn't last. At 10:35 P.M., on September 19, 1881, President James Abram Garfield died. Fourteen-year-old Mary wrote in her diary:

In his New York City home, Vice President Chester A. Arthur (second from right) took the oath of office in 1881 in front of a justice of the New York State Supreme Court.

—————————— ✧

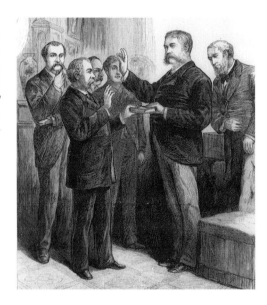

"We got Papa out of hot Washington, & took him to Elberon, where for the first few days he seemed to rally, but it was merely temporary . . . oh! it is so hard to lose him."

A little after midnight, Vice President Arthur received a telegram from cabinet members asking him to take the oath of office without delay. John Brady, a state supreme court judge, administered the oath in Arthur's parlor at 2:15 A.M.

After an autopsy, which incorrectly stated that Garfield had died of internal bleeding rather than massive infection, his body lay in state at the Capitol. A private burial took place at Cleveland's Lake View Cemetery, not far from where Garfield first yearned to be a sailor.

Charles Guiteau's two-month trial started on November 14. Guiteau pleaded insanity before a packed courtroom. He argued that his shots were not fatal and that "the Deity

The court interviewed more than 131 prospective jurors to find 12 for Guiteau's trial for Garfield's murder. The trial lasted 71 days. But the jury met for less than one hour before finding Guiteau guilty and sentencing him to death by hanging.

───────── ✧

[God]," through allowing medical incompetence and other circumstances, had killed Garfield. Guiteau had stalked Garfield several times and had almost shot him in June when the president and his wife left for Elberon. But he decided that he could not kill Garfield in front of Lucretia.

Guiteau claimed that he "sought to remove" Garfield, because of his "duty to the Lord and to the American people." He had considered Garfield his political friend and had expected "an important office" from him. When the president forced Stalwart leader Roscoe Conkling from the Senate, Guiteau realized that the U.S. political system was in danger. He believed Chester Arthur would restore things to their proper order.

The jury found Guiteau guilty. President Arthur rejected a petition from 160 doctors who claimed Guiteau was insane. Guiteau was hanged at a Washington, D.C., jail on June 30, 1882.

MEDICINE

The bullet that entered James A. Garfield on July 2, 1881, fractured one of his ribs, shattered a lumbar vertebra, missed his spinal cord, and lodged near his pancreas. Medical historians think that the president might have recovered from these injuries if his attending doctors had washed their hands before examining him and had used sterilized instruments.

In Garfield's time, the theory that germs caused fatal infections was not universally accepted. Earlier, British researcher Joseph Lister showed that cleaning wounds and protecting them from germs saved lives. But as late as 1879, a leading London surgeon thought that the appearance of "laudable [praiseworthy] pus"—a sign of infection—meant that healing was occurring within the body. One doctor consulting on Garfield's case, D. Hayes Agnew, favored Lister's treatment of wounds. But even Dr. Agnew did not totally understand the theory of antisepsis (prevention of infection).

Most of Garfield's doctors were allopaths, who believed in treating disease aggressively with medicines that combat the disease directly. For example, using antibiotics such as

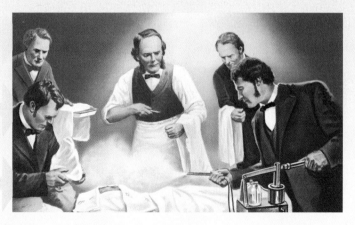

◈ ——————

British researcher Joseph Lister (center) directs use of an antiseptic spray (right) in a surgical demonstration in 1867.

An ordinary citizen (left) gives a remedy for President Garfield to an armed guard at the White House. In 1854 Dr. Susan Edson (right), Lucretia Garfield's doctor, had been one of the first women to graduate from Cleveland Homeopathic College in Cleveland, Ohio.

penicillin to kill bacterial infections comes from the allopathic tradition. Two of the doctors—Garfield's cousin, Silas Boynton, and Lucretia Garfield's doctor, Susan Edson—believed in homeopathic medicine. In homeopathy, "like cures like." The patient often takes a very small quantity of a substance that produces a reaction in the body, which rids the body of a disease. Vaccinations come from the homeopathic tradition.

Garfield and his wife thought that homeopathic doctors were at least as important to medicine as allopathic doctors. When Garfield was in Congress, he supported a bill to establish equal rights in government hiring and service to both types of doctors. But the allopathic doctors opposed the bill, and it was defeated.

This collage of photos from the Garfield assassination includes portraits of Garfield (top), his doctors Bliss (left) and Townshend (right), and his assassin Guiteau (bottom). Photos of the railroad depot where the assassination took place (an exterior view, center, and interior views, top left and right); Garfield's coffin on display at the U.S. Capitol (bottom left); and Guiteau's gun (bottom right) are also shown.

✧ ————————

HISTORICAL PHOTOGRAPH
OF THE
ASSASSINATION OF PRESIDENT GARFIELD.

Entered according to act of Congress, in the year 1881, by C. M. BELL,
in the office of the Librarian of Congress, at Washington, D. C.

Garfield's mother, Eliza, died six years later. Lucretia Garfield moved back to Ohio and never remarried. Congress granted her a pension. Including money earned from investments, Lucretia lived comfortably at the farm in Mentor and in a house in Cleveland. With help from her late husband's secretary, Joseph Stanley Brown, she organized Garfield's papers into the nation's first presidential library.

On June 14, 1888, Mary Garfield married Joseph Stanley Brown, and Harry married Belle Mason. Both weddings were at the house in Mentor. Lucretia died in 1918.

Harry became a president of Williams College and lived until 1942. Mary became active in civic associations in New York, where her husband was an investment banker and editor at the National Geographic Society. She died in 1947. James, who died in 1950, worked in the U.S. Civil Service Commission and served as secretary of the interior for President Theodore Roosevelt. Irvin, a lawyer, died in 1951. Abram, who was only eight when his father was shot, became an architect. He died in 1958.

Six years before his death, Garfield wrote in his journal about raising children and added: "We ought to live one preliminary life in order to know how to live the real one." We don't know what James A. Garfield would have done differently if he could have lived another life or what he might have accomplished during a longer term as president. But we do know that his assassination led Congress in 1883 to pass the Pendleton Act. That act firmly established the type of merit-based civil service Garfield worked for and we now have. It is a fitting legacy for a man who spent nearly half of his forty-nine years in the service of his country.

TIMELINE

1831   James Abram Garfield is born in Orange Township, Ohio, on November 19.

1833   Abram Garfield (father) dies.

1848   James Garfield becomes a canal boy on the *Evening Star.*

1849   Garfield begins classes at Geauga Academy.

1850   Garfield joins the Disciples of Christ Church and begins preaching. He enters Western Reserve Eclectic Institute (Hiram College).

1854   Garfield enters Williams College.

1856   Garfield graduates from Williams and joins the faculty at Eclectic Institute.

1857   Garfield becomes president of Eclectic Institute.

1858   Garfield marries Lucretia "Crete" Rudolph on November 11.

1859   Garfield is elected to the Ohio Senate.

1860   Elizabeth "Trot" Garfield is born on July 3.

1861   Garfield becomes a lawyer. He volunteers for the Union army and leads troops in Kentucky and Tennessee.

1862   Garfield is elected to the U.S. House of Representatives.

1863   Garfield is promoted to major general. Harry Garfield is born on October 11. "Trot" Garfield dies on December 1.

1865   James Rudolph Garfield is born on October 17.

1867   Mary "Mollie" Garfield is born on January 17.

1869 Garfield becomes chairman of the House Committee on Banking and Commerce.

1870 Irvin McDowell Garfield is born on August 3, 1870.

1871 Garfield becomes chairman of the House Committee on Appropriations.

1872 Garfield negotiates a treaty with the Salish (Flathead) Nation. Abram Garfield is born on November 12.

1877 Garfield is appointed to an electoral committee in the Tilden-Hayes dispute. The committee appoints Hayes president.

1878 Garfield becomes minority leader in the U.S. House of Representatives.

1880 Garfield is elected U.S. senator on January 13. He is elected president on November 2.

1881 Garfield is sworn in as president on March 4. He is shot by Charles Guiteau on July 2 and dies in Elberon, New Jersey, on September 19.

SOURCE NOTES

7 Theodore Clarke Smith, *The Life and Letters of James Abram Garfield* (New Haven, CT: Yale University Press, 1925), 1:27.

7 Harlan Hatcher, *The Western Reserve: The Story of New Connecticut in Ohio* (New York: The Bobbs-Merrill Company, Inc., 1949), 113.

7 Theodore Clarke Smith, 1:22.

8 Ibid., 24.

8 Ibid., 25.

9 Ibid., 18.

10 Theodore Clarke Smith, 1:5.

11 Ibid., 12–13.

15 Ibid.

16 Ibid., 19.

16 Ibid., 20.

16 Ibid.

17 Ibid., 23.

17 Ibid.

18 Ibid., 26.

18 Ibid.

18 Ibid., 18.

19 Ibid., 73.

19 Ibid., 35.

19 Ibid., 36.

20 Ibid., 29.

21 Ibid.

21 Ibid., 30.

24 Hatcher, 18.

25 Ibid., 41.

25 Ibid., 51.

25 Ibid., 54.

26 Ibid., 62.

27 Ibid., 74.

28 Ibid., 101.

30 Ibid., 123.

30 Ibid., 126.

30 Theodore Clarke Smith, 2:821.

31 Ibid., 1:142.

32 Ibid., 237.

33 Ibid., 150.

33 Ibid., 152.

34 Ibid., 155.

34 Ibid., 161.

34 Ibid.

35 Ibid., 162.

38 Ibid., 209.

39 Ridpath, 117.

39 Ibid.

40 Henry Steele Commager, *Documents of American History*, 7th ed. (New York: Appleton-Century-Crofts, 1963), 420.

40 Theodore Clarke Smith, 1:245.

41 Dee Lillegard, *James A. Garfield* (Chicago: Children's Press, 1987), 43.

42 Ibid., 353.

44 Theodore Clarke Smith, 2:705.

45 John Clark Ridpath, *The Life and Work of James A. Garfield, Twentieth President of the United States* (Cincinnati: Jones Brothers and Co., 1882), 194.

46 James A. Garfield, "A Century of Congress," *Atlantic Monthly*, July 1877, 62.

50 Theodore Clarke Smith, 2:780.

53 Commager, 493.

54 "First Inaugural Address of Ulysses S. Grant," *The Avalon Project at Yale Law School,* 1997, http://www.yale.edu/lawweb/avalon/presiden/inaug/grant1.htm (December 17, 2004).

57 Theodore Clarke Smith, 1:465.

58 Ibid., 488.

58 Ibid., 728.

58 Ibid.

59 Kenneth D. Ackerman, *Dark Horse: The Surprise Election and Political Murder of President James A. Garfield* (New York: Carroll & Graf Publishers, 2003), 149.

59 Theodore Clarke Smith, 2:926.

60–61 Theodore Clarke Smith, 1:541.

61 Ibid., 547–548.

64 Ibid., 564.
64 Ibid., 505.
64 Ibid., 514.
65 Ibid., 582.
66 Garfield, 63.
66–67 Commager, 536.
67 Ibid., 587.
70 Theodore Clarke Smith, 2:918.
71 Ibid., 1:615.
75 Howard Zinn, *A People's History of the United States,* Twentieth Anniversary Edition (New York: HarperCollins Publishers, 1999), 245.
76–77 Page Smith, *The Rise of Industrial America,* vol. 6, *A People's History of the Post-Reconstruction Era* (New York: McGraw-Hill Book Company, 1984), 187.
80 Ackerman, 37–38.
80 Ibid., 38.
82 Ibid., 133.
83 Page Smith, 118.
85 "Inaugural Address of James A. Garfield," *The Avalon Project at Yale Law School,* 1997, http://www.yale.edu/lawweb/avalon/presiden/inaug/garfield.htm (December 17, 2004).
85–86 Ibid.
86 Ibid.
86 Ackerman, 286.
86 Ibid., 268.
86 Ibid.
87 Ibid., 278.
90 Theodore Clarke Smith, 2:1169.
94 Ackerman, 379.
94 James C. Clark, *The Murder of James A. Garfield: The President's Last Days and the Trial and Execution of His Assassin* (Jefferson, NC: McFarland & Company, Inc., 1993), 60.
94 Ackerman, 405.
97 Clark, 107.
98 Lillegard, 86.
98–99 Clark, 123.
99 Ibid.
99 Ibid.
99 Ibid.
100 Clark, 70.
101 Ibid., 74.
103 Theodore Clarke Smith, 2:923.

SELECTED BIBLIOGRAPHY

Ackerman, Kenneth D. *Dark Horse: The Surprise Election and Political Murder of President James A. Garfield.* New York: Carroll & Graf Publishers, 2003.

Clark, James C. *The Murder of James A. Garfield: The President's Last Days and the Trial and Execution of His Assassin.* Jefferson, NC: McFarland & Company, Inc., 1993.

Commager, Henry Steele. *Documents of American History.* 7th ed. New York: Appleton-Century-Crofts, 1963.

Everds, John. *The Spectacular Trains: A History of Rail Transportation.* Northbrook, Il: Hubbard Press, 1973.

Garfield, James A. "A Century of Congress," *Atlantic Monthly,* July 1877.

Hatcher, Harlan. *The Western Reserve: The Story of New Connecticut in Ohio.* New York: The Bobbs-Merrill Company, Inc., 1949.

"Inaugural Address of James A. Garfield," *The Avalon Project at Yale Law School,* 1997. http://www.yale.edu/lawweb/avalon/presiden/ inaug/garfield.htm (December 17, 2004).

Masur, Louis P. *1831: Year of Eclipse.* New York: Hill and Wang, 2001.

Rhodes, James F. *History of the United States from the Compromise of 1850 to the McKinley-Bryan Campaign of 1896.* Vol. 6. Port Washington, NY: Kennekat Press, Inc., 1906.

Ridpath, John Clark. *The Life and Work of James A. Garfield, Twentieth President of the United States.* Cincinnati: Jones Brothers and Co., 1882.

Smith, Page. *The Rise of Industrial America:* Vol.6, *A People's History of the Post-Reconstruction Era.* New York: McGraw-Hill Book Company, 1984.

Smith, Theodore Clarke, ed. *The Life and Letters of James Abram Garfield.* 2 vols. New Haven, CT: Yale University Press, 1925.

FURTHER READING AND WEBSITES

Brunelli, Carol. *James A. Garfield, Our Twentieth President.* Chanhassen, MN: The Child's World, Inc., 2002.

Green, Meg. *Into the Land of Freedom.* Minneapolis: Lerner Publications Company, 2004.

Hakim, Joy. *Reconstructing America.* 3rd ed. New York: Oxford University Press, 2003.

Havelin, Kate. *Andrew Johnson.* Minneapolis: Lerner Publications Company, 2005.

———*Ulysses S. Grant.* Minneapolis: Lerner Publications Company, 2005.

Heinrichs, Ann. *Lucretia Rudolph Garfield: 1832–1918.* Chicago: Children's Press, 1998.

"Inaugural Address of James A. Garfield." *The Avalon Project at Yale Law School,* http://www.yale.edu/lawweb/avalon/presiden/inaug/garfield.htm Read James Garfield's inaugural address at the Avalon Project at Yale Law School website. It features documents in law, history, and diplomacy, including the inaugural speeches of U.S. presidents.

"James A. Garfield National Historic Site" *National Park Service,* http://www.nps.gov/jaga This Web page describes the James A. Garfield National Historic Site in Mentor, Ohio. The page includes details about visiting and how to e-mail the site for additional information.

Lillegard, Dee. *James A. Garfield.* Chicago: Children's Press, 1987.

"Lucretia Rudolph Garfield," *The White House,* http://www.whitehouse.gov/history/firstladies/lg20.html This site features information on First Lady Lucretia Rudolph Garfield.

Western Reserve Historical Society, http://www.wrhs.org This site has information on the Western Reserve—the part of Ohio in which James Garfield was born.

Williams, John Hoyt. *A Great & Shining Road: The Epic Story of the Transcontinental Railroad.* New York: Times Books, 1988.

INDEX

rights, 85–86; and Reconstruction, 44, 46–47, 53; Red Cross, 89; relieved of duty, 39; and Rutherford B. Hayes, 68–71, 74–75, 76–77; as sailor, 7–8, 16–18; and slavery, 28, 30, 34, 38, 39, 40, 44, 47–48, 56, 85–86; and the Smithsonian Institution, 56; the Star Routes fraud, 90; as state senator, 30–31, 32, 33; teen years, 13–16; and Thomas Edison, 83; and Ulysses S. Grant, 38, 56–57, 64, 67, 71, 80–81, 90, 93; as U.S. Representative, 38, 40, 41, 43, 53–54, 55–58, 60–61, 63; as U.S. Senator, 78–83; Western Reserve Eclectic Institute (Hiram College), 23–24, 26, 28; and Williams College, 26–28, 92

Garfield, James Rudolph (son), 45, 49, 67, 79, 90, 91, 93, 94, 103

Garfield, Mary (sister), 9, 11, 12, 13, 26

Garfield, Mary "Mollie" (daughter), 48, 90, 91, 93–94, 98, 103

Garfield, Mehitabel "Hitty" (sister), 9, 11–12, 13

Garfield, Rudolph, Lucretia "Crete" (wife), 24, 26, 28–29, 32, 35, 38, 40, 42–43, 44, 52, 54, 59, 61, 67, 71, 79, 80, 82; as first lady, 90–91, 93, 94, 101, 102

Garfield, Thomas (brother), 9, 11–12, 13, 18, 25

Grant, Ulysses S.; 44, 45, 52–53, 54–57, 63, 66, 67–68; and James A. Garfield, 38, 56–57, 64, 67, 71, 80–81, 90, 93

Greenback Party, 68–69; and 1876 Presidential Election, 70–71

Guiteau, Charles, 86–87; as assassin, 94, 102; trial of, 98–99

Hayes, Rutherford B. 68, 83; and James A. Garfield, 68–71, 74–75, 76–77; and Star Routes scandal, 90

Hinsdale, Burke A., 82; and correspondence with James A. Garfield, 41, 64, 65, 66, 71

Johnson, Andrew, 45, 46; impeachment of, 52–54, 56; and Reconstruction, 47–52

Lincoln, Abraham, 33, 34–35, 40, 62; and assassination of, 45, 46; and the Emancipation Proclamation, 40; and James A. Garfield, 43, 44

Lincoln, Robert Todd, 88; and Garfield assassination, 94

Native Americans, 24, 63; and James A. Garfield, 58

railroads, 57, 60, 64; and James A. Garfield, 38, 62–63, 97, 102; and workers' strike, 76–77

Reconstruction, 44–45, 47–52, 53, 54, 55, 60, 66, 75

Republican Party, 40, 43, 64, 79, 81, 82; and James A. Garfield, 30, 38, 47, 88; and Radicals, 66; and Stalwarts, 80

Rosencrans, William, and James A. Garfield, 41–43

slavery and slaves, 20, 28, 38, 39; freed and former slaves (freedmen), 46–48, 49, 56, 57, 75. *See also* African Americans

Stevens, Thaddeus, 53; and James A. Garfield, 47, 49, 56

Tilden, Samuel, 83; and 1876 Presidential Election, 68, 71, 74

Tuttle, G. N., and 1876 Presidential Election, 70–71

U.S. Constitution, 54, 67, 72, 74, 86, 88; and Fifteenth Amendment to, 54, 55; and Fourteenth Amendment to, 47–49; and Thirteenth Amendment to, 44, 47

Western Reserve, 24, 39

ABOUT THE AUTHOR

Ruth Tenzer Feldman has written several books on U.S. history and a biography of Thurgood Marshall. She is also a regular contributor to *Cobblestone* and *Odyssey* magazines. Feldman grew up in Long Branch, New Jersey, not far from where James Garfield died, and became a legislative attorney for the U.S. Department of Education, which Garfield proposed while he was in Congress. She lives in Bethesda, Maryland, with her husband, her Welsh corgi, and a trusty computer. You can find out more about her and contact her through www.ruthtenzerfeldman.com.

PHOTO ACKNOWLEDGMENTS

The images in this book are used with the permission of: The White House, pp. 1, 7, 9, 19, 32, 46, 66, 85; Library of Congress, pp. 2 (LC-DIG-cwpbh-04855), 15 (LC-USZ62-110084), 21 (LC-USZC2-2465), 26 (LC-USZ62-100087), 29 (LC-DIG-ggbain-03485), 34 (LC-USZC4-528), 35 (Geography and Map Collection), 36 (LC-DIG-cwpbh-01154), 37 (LC-DIG-cwpbh-06455), 40 (LC-USZ62-2070), 42 (LC-USZC4-2540), 48 (LC-USZ62-913442), 51, 52 (LC-DIG-cwpb-06437), 53 (LC-USZ62-106848), 55 (LC-USZC4-2399), 59 (LC-DIG-cwpbh-04026), 62 (LC-USZ62-116354), 65 (LC-USZ62-56429), 69 (LC-USZ62-37424), 70 (HABS, OHIO, 43-MENT,2-2), 74 (LC-USZ62-97512), 76 (LC-USZ62-18145), 78 (LC-USZ6-823), 80 (LC-DIG-cwpbh-05176), 82 (LC-USZ62-112153), 83 (LC-DIG-cwpbh-03741), 84 (LC-USZ6-55), 87, 88 (LC-DIG-cwpbh-04781) 91 (LC-USZ62-129832), 95 (LC-USZ62-104275), 97 (LC-USZ62-124389), 98 (USZ62-7615), 101 both (LC-USZ62-104052), 102 (LC-USZ62-80339); Cornell University Library, Making of America Digital Collection, p. 6; © Brown Brothers, pp. 10, 13, 17, 31, 81, 92, 99; © Granger Collection, New York, p. 14; © Northwind Picture Archives, pp. 23, 27, 61; © CORBIS, pp. 33, 50; © Bettmann/CORBIS, pp. 77, 100; American Red Cross, 89.

Cover: Library of Congress (LC-DIG-cwpbh-03744)